D1583083

Glassforming

A HISTORY OF
Glassforming

KEITH CUMMINGS

A & C BLACK • LONDON
UNIVERSITY OF PENNSYLVANIA PRESS • PHILADELPHIA

First published in Great Britain 2002 by
A & C Black (Publishers) Limited
Alderman House
37 Soho Square
London W1D 3QZ

ISBN 0-7136-5274-8

Published simultaneously in the USA by
the University of Pennsylvania Press
4200 Pine Street, Philadelphia,
Pennsylvania 19104–4011

ISBN 0-8122-3647-5

CIP catalogue records for this book are available from the British Library and the U.S. Library of Congress

Printed and bound in Singapore by Tien Wah Press (Pte.) Ltd

FRONT COVER ILLUSTRATIONS: (CLOCKWISE FROM TOP LEFT)
Pressed, iridesced tile by Tiffany; handmade marbles by Greg Beeten; tile by Tiffany; detail of vase by Alvar Aalto, 1937; lampworking
using pre-formed rod; detail of *The Embassy Suite* by Frank Hill and designed by H. Powell at Whitefriers in 1938; tile by Tiffany; a
Bullseye hand-rolled sheet of glass; tile by Tiffany

BACK COVER ILLUSTRATION:
Fragments series vessel, by Joel Philip Myers

SPINE ILLUSTRATION:
Islamic water-sprinkler from the 18th century

Designed by Penny and Tony Mills
Cover design by Dorothy Moir

I should like to thank all of the museums, collections and individuals who have made it possible for me to
include material held by them in this volume. Particularly:

Derek Balmer, Barbara Beadman of Plowden and Thompson Ltd., Cathie Currie of Pilchuck, Dr. Susan Dawes of the
University of Central England, Roger Dodsworth of Broadfield House Glass Museum, Janet Elliott, Victoria Emmanuel of
Birmingham Museum and Art Gallery, Stuart Garfoot, Dudley F. Giberson, Sue Giles of Bristol Museum and Art Gallery,
Michael Glancy, Theresa Green of the British Glass Manufacturers Federation, Warren Langley, John Lewis, Brett Littman of
Urban Glass Quarterly, Lani McGregor of Bullseye Glass, Julie McMaster of Toledo Museum of Art, Rick Mills, Joel Myers,
Jean-Luc Olivie of the Centre du Verre in Paris, David Redman, Colin Reid, Jennifer Rennie of Hawarth Art Gallery, in
Accrington, Schott Glass, Paul Stankard, Dinah Stobbs of Pilkington Archive, and Bertil Vallien.

Contents

'The maker and the object made reacted upon the other. Until modern times, apart from the esoteric knowledge of the priests, philosophers and astronomers the greater part of human thought and imagination flowed through the hands.'

Lewis Mumford, *The Myth of the Machine: Technics and Human Development*, London, 1967.

Introduction

'there are discovered underlying and valid reasons which retrospectively confer an apparent
necessity upon the effective outcome. It is forgotten that the opposite outcome might perhaps
have permitted an equally satisfactory explanation …'

Raymond Aron, *Introduction to the Philosophy of History*,
Boston, 1961.

Given the nature of this book, the way I have selected my examples and my reasons for taking a particular viewpoint of them, I feel that it is necessary to introduce and, to a certain extent, justify my approach.

In deciding to present an account of the history and development of glassforming processes I have limited myself to those that take as their starting point glass as a mobile, supercooled liquid whose precise viscosity can be triggered and controlled by heat. This effectively restricts my account to processes that build, shape or transform glass by the way they choose to react to its mobile states.

It also, by definition, precludes from this study those processes that shape glass through the abrasion of it as a cold, static solid: grinding, cutting, engraving, sand blasting and polishing. My justification for this large omission is not based on value judgements of either the importance of cold processes or of the qualities they impart to glass formed through them. Historically, there has always existed a natural organic division between hot and cold glass processes. The Romans firmly divided glass workers into those who formed glass hot (*Vitrearii*) and those who shaped it cold (*Diatrearii*). Reductive processes that removed cold, solid glass through abrasion had a different evolution, invariably being adapted from existing technologies that had been developed originally for shaping other materials, usually hard stones. These processes belong, in terms of their creative pedigree, to the histories of sculpture, jewellery or lapidary: they were not developed for glass and their history in relation to it is one of

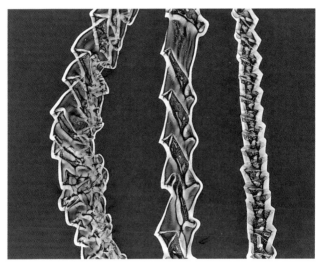

An illustration of the mobile, dual nature of hot liquid glass, frozen into its form and surface during its rapid reduction from 1100°C to room temperature. The poured stream of glass folds as it hits a flat surface, but the rigid nature of the outside skin prevents it from simply pooling and helps to create a permanent record of its movements.

(OPPOSITE PAGE)

A Roman Modulus: a wine measure and drinking vessel. Created in response to practical requirements, the form of this type of object is often the result of a gradual process of change. Although by anonymous makers, such artefacts have immense presence and style, and despite the fact that their original forms derive from ceramic or metal models, the basic elements are expressed in terms of the material of glass.

Photo, Derek Balmer.

adaptation. The great seventeenth-century engraver Caspar Lehmann, who established the European school of relief engraving, began his career as a gem engraver and only turned to glass in the middle of his career. Without such lateral movement of course, glass would have developed in a totally different form, and we would be much the poorer for it. However, the account I have attempted to assemble and present has at its centre the unique and contradictory viscous material known as glass, and describes brilliant and individual creative reactions to, and partnerships with, this particular form of the material. I do not believe it has been presented in quite this format before and it is, in my opinion, more than enough for one volume.

We experience glass very much in terms of its usage: in the form of objects, artefacts, devices, apparatus, and as a building material. Much of our appreciation of glass, and view of it as a material, is determined by our use and perception of these end products. Its particular material qualities can even cause it to determine the name of the end product, for example we drink from a 'glass'. Because of the way in which we encounter glass products, as commodities or fixtures, the mysteries that surround their manufacture remain both unknown and inaccessible. Where access to glass making is permitted the impact on the consumer can be profound. Glassblowing, for example, has recently encouraged such visual access as a positive marketing aid. As Gloria Hickey points out, 'Buyers can witness the process of the object's creation. In fact glassblowers have lamented that they cannot sell the molten glass object because a buyer will often request "the one on the pipe".'[1]

Any account of hot glass processes, no matter how thorough, would only present a partial view of humankind's five-thousand-year relationship with its first synthetic material creation. No glass object, whether a work of art, a lens, a window or mass produced container, arrived at its precise form and function by the following of a laid down, inevitable, logical path. Each particular form and use of glass in the world is rather the heir to an evolution, fuelled by the relationship forged between its material properties, its behaviour when heated and a series of wonderfully inventive reactions to these by individuals. In our era we can name such individuals, Michael Owens, for example, and describe their

A pressed-glass bust of the self-taught American genius Michael Owens, who designed and developed the first fully automatic bottle-making machine. It seems entirely fitting that the precise amount of hot glass needed to fill this mould was gathered from the mass of hot glass in the furnace by his own unique suction device.

Science Museum Picture Library, London.

particular contribution, but the vast majority are and will remain anonymous; yet our ability to use glass in such diverse ways is totally dependant on their accumulated insights. Fortunately, the story can be related even though most of its chief protagonists cannot be named. This then is an attempt to describe this partnership, and particularly of the important roles played by adverse and unwelcome factors. Problems that added to the already difficult task of mixing, founding and working glass often brought from people a creative response that yielded, in the long run, a beneficial result.

Three main themes dominate the story: (1) the search for a particular product, glass sheet, for example (2) the search for specific versions of the material, particularly the long denied goal of colourless, crystal-like glass, and (3) the search for a way round a problem, for instance a way of compensating for the loss of access to a traditional source of raw constituent and the need for an acceptable substitute. Each solution involved a spark

of intuition allied to often massive investments in time, energy and often money. Sometimes success was gradual, the result of an accumulation of small improvements added over many generations; at other times it was achieved quickly by individuals or small groups who could think round, beyond and sideways from accepted practice. People like Michael Owens, who invented the bottle-making machine; Bernard Perrot, who isolated sheet glass manufacture as a problem separate from glass blowing; and Pierre

The manufacture of optical glass c. 1930. Electrically operated mechanical arms extend into each pot of molten glass, and rotate while the glass is founding. This has the effect of homogenising the mixture and, by the constant folding action, creates a glass without blemishes, suitable for use in optics. Like many mechanised glass procedures this mimics a manual activity devised for the same purpose.

In direct contrast to the Roman wine vessel shown opposite the beginning of this introduction this is a product that is the result of a conscious set of design decisions, made in response to the forces of economics, process and marketing. The advantage of using a named designer is twofold: he has the ability to respond to this kind of brief in an original way, and the end product can be sold as a signature item, reflecting the designer's particular style. Material and process are utilised to contribute to the nature of the product, particularly in terms of ease of mass production.

Designer, Stuart Garfoot.

Guinand, who achieved the breakthrough in optical glass production by transferring his experience from metallurgy to glass.

All objects, particularly those that serve a predominantly practical function, are the result of some sort of compromise between a set of contradictory pressures. The needs of commerce, repeatability, practicality, material and style, to name but a few parts of the complex network of pressures within which an object must evolve. In the case of vernacular forms, such as the Roman Modulus shown at the beginning of the chapter, this process is a gradual, continuous, evolutionary and largely unselfconscious process, whereas in an industrially developed society it is a selfconscious design process (see above and p.5).

If such a set of pressures can be described as an equation of forces, then a major element of this equation must be the nature and behaviour of glass, with often the best objects being those which use the materials qualities to produce a solution to the whole range of requirements for success. Glass is, of course, itself a human construct, a mixture of ordinary common materials synthesised through heat to create an extraordinary, uncommon one. Although it is a synthetic, its original development, at least 5000 years ago, must have been a haphazard affair based on accident, observation and practical experiments. The scientific basis for the understanding of its nature did not begin until the eighteenth century and is still far from complete. As Susan Frank says 'Glass is one of the most complex of substances, its scientific study as a disordered, multi-component system is in many ways still in its infancy.'[2]

The original design drawing for the range illustrated on p.4. An essential element of designed objects, such drawings help to plan and direct the production process, including the crucial decision to produce the item at all. Drawings, models and prototypes all play a part in this system, and clearly a design that utilises the natural qualities of a material is an asset.
Designer, Stuart Garfoot.

Glass is a complex and difficult material to make and understand, yet throughout the bulk of its history it was made successfully without really being understood in scientific terms. This was achieved by a concentration on the fruitful circumstances of its producing, often accidentally achieved, and through the operation of ritual folklore and a linear, hands-on tradition ensuring their repeatability in a workable form. Its conversion into a scientifically understood and controllable entity occupies only a fraction of its five-thousand-year existence, albeit one that coincides with our era. This has merely allowed glass to extend its range through our greater control of it.

Ancient processes were part of their respective cultures and were used to make objects that remain unsurpassed in our own, despite our technological advances. This is why this is a book with a narrative theme rather than a dictionary of processes and techniques. As such it cannot be exhaustive but attempts to present an introduction to, and an understanding of the general principles behind the main processes, their historical evolution and their crucial role in determining how glass objects themselves took the forms they did.

I hope that my account will add something to the appreciation of a material that has involved and fascinated me as a teacher and maker for forty years. Above all, I would like this book to pay tribute to the contributions of the artisans, makers, inventors, engineers and entrepreneurs who, by their individual creativity, helped to steer the development of glass in the diverse directions it has taken, and which ensure that its story will continue as long as mankind.

CHAPTER ONE

The Nature of the Material

'We are very much controlled by what we can do. We tend to avoid things that are too difficult
for us; if we can solve certain equations, we tend to go that way.'
Sir Fred Hoyle, quoted in *A Brief History of Time, a Reader's Companion*,
G. Stove, London, 1992

Our current knowledge concerning the origins of glass is partial and confused, but it is still possible to speculate about how its peculiar behavioural properties affected the way humankind approached the problem of how to form it. The above quotation, of Professor Hoyle, is a comment about the way in which our search for knowledge is driven by what we already possess and towards that which we feel is nearest to our grasp, and it could quite easily have been intended to describe the historical development of glassforming. The major theme of this book is that an examination of glass objects as isolated end products does not reveal the roles of insight, experiment and refinement that preceded their manufacture, to say nothing about the way in which each type of object evolved through a process of trial and error, often spread over many decades. To put it bluntly, the way in which definitive examples of high-quality glass artefacts are displayed and presented in books or museums obscures the fact that they only occurred in their final form at the end of a journey that was often haphazard and far from logical. Object and process are linked into a creative dependency, for each new generation can only choose to react to that which it inherits, and it is in the nature of this reaction that progress lies. The nature of the classic eighteenth-century wineglass, for example, with its generic bowl, foot and stem, seems to embody an inner formal logic that has established this arrangement as the standard form for a drinking glass. Yet its origins reveal that its form evolved out of

The 'Saga' range of wineglasses, designed by Stuart Garfoot for Rosenthal. Although produced by mass-production methods, its form displays the classic, traditional elements – bowl, foot and stem. This evolved relationship of separate parts has become the standard wineglass format.

Courtesy Stuart Garfoot.

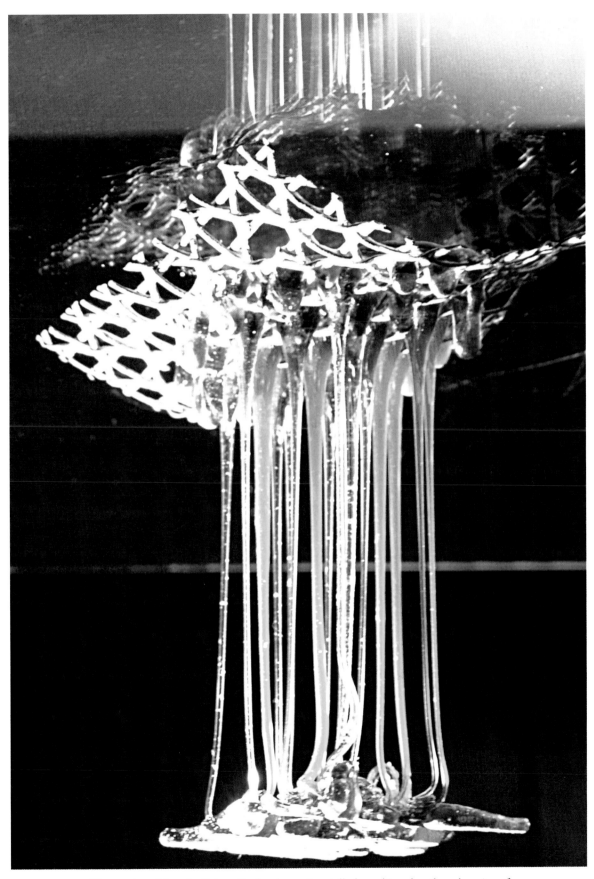

The creation of threads of glass. Produced experimentally by melting glass through a piece of perforated metal in a kiln. See glass fibre production on p.19

A drinking vessel whose form reflects precisely the habits of the culture it served. This required a glass to be held in the hand while it contained liquid. It also gave us the term 'tumbler'.
Photo, Derek Balmer.

Window-glass strengthened with wire, showing the effects of a fire; glass, which is frozen into a solid at room temperature, becomes distorted when re-heated. The wire mesh embedded in the glass has restricted the melting caused by heat.
Pilkington Bros Ltd Archive.

an attempt by the culture to modify forms it had inherited from another. The unstable 'tumbler' of the European and Eastern Dark Ages was produced in response to a social code that dictated that a drinking vessel should remain in the hand until empty: any attempt to put the tumbler down when full would result in spillage. This cone like form (see previous page), itself derived in the West from animal horns, was inherited by the Venetians but had to be made stable to function within a new set of social fashions. The decision to place the bowl on a stem and foot

was an inspired one which created the classic format, which remains, in essence, unchanged today. History rarely allows us the luxury of devising anything from scratch without reference to the past.

What is true of glass products is equally true of the material and its processes. An examination of the way in which the major glassforming technologies have evolved over five thousand years reveals that process or families of processes relate to, and often derive from, a particular characteristic of glass as a raw workable material.

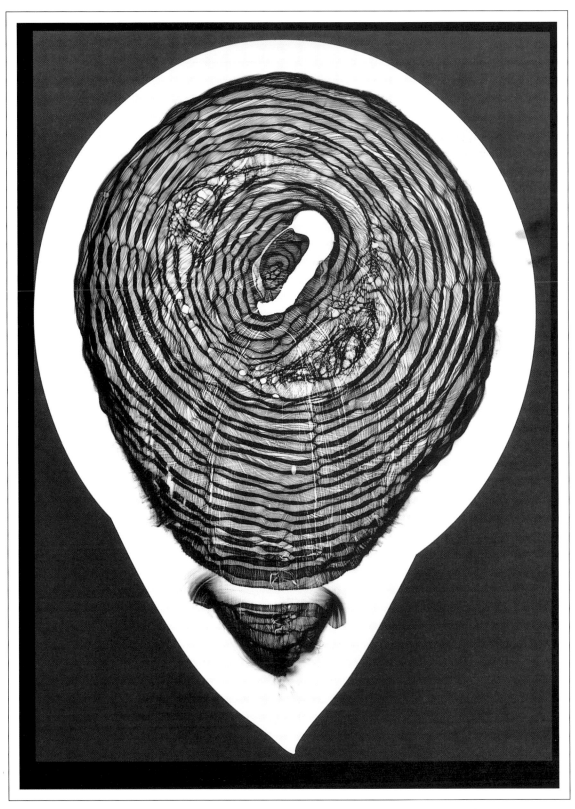

A graphic illustration of the essential relationship between the interior glass mass and its surface skin. The way in which the skin hardens and contracts in contrast with the warmer, more mobile interior is revealed by the concentric ridges or riffles frozen into its surface, and the mark left by the shears as they cut through the glass to separate it from the mass on the gathering iron. Any hot glassforming process has to take these special behavioural characteristics into primary consideration.

Glass is anything but a neutral partner and can only ever be worked effectively when its peculiarities and limitations are recognised and creatively harnessed.

Despite the differences between the many processes that are used to shape glass through heat they all share a common starting point. This starting point is the prime characteristic of glass as a unique material, and without it not only would the material display different properties but the range of forming procedures could not have evolved.

HEAT AND LIQUIDITY

There are two constant truths central to the synthesis and primary shaping of glass, whatever its eventual properties and use: heat and viscosity.

Heat is a pre-requisite for the existence of glass, as it is required to melt and synthesise the basic ingredients i.e. silica, stabiliser and flux, into the new, unique unity that is glass. Once cooled it becomes solid; it is actually a supercooled or frozen liquid in terms of its essential structure. This liquidity is based on a sliding scale relative to heat: crudely speaking, the hotter glass gets the more liquid it becomes. Generally speaking, it is this liquidity, triggered by selected heat levels, that forms the basis of its primary shaping processes.

Even as a viscous liquid it does not behave exactly as a liquid should and until recently scientists created a fourth state of matter to encompass its contradictory behaviour, 'the glassy state'. The two major characteristics of glass as a liquid are that its viscosity can be determined, and as it cools it creates an elastic boundary skin at its junction with air. (see p.10) The interaction of these two characteristics forms the basis for *all* heat-based procedures. The fact that this interaction of skin and mass is contradictory has allowed the development of forming processes that are unique to glass. The relationship that exists between the mobile, liquid mass of the glass and the elastic skin permits strange, anomalous procedures like the shearing of a liquid or processes like toughening where the interior mass of the glass is in compression and the skin is in tension, with both forces engineered to exist in equilibrium (see right).[3]

Although all glass processes have developed

Two rapidly cooled 'drops' of glass, made by pouring molten glass into water. They are a perfect example of the relationship between the interior mass of glass and the exterior skin. Because of the rapid cooling, the skin is in tension and the interior is in compression; this is the principle behind toughened glass, and such drops are, in one sense, immensely strong. The head of the drop can sustain blows from a hammer, whilst the tiniest pressure on the tail breaks the skin and results in an explosive shattering of the whole drop. These Prince Rupert drops, named after Prince Rupert of Bavaria, provided amusement as novelties after their discovery in the 18th century.

Science Museum Picture Library, London.

through their creative relationship with this duality, the ways in which this has been negotiated are varied. It is worth looking at the main processes with special reference to this point of contact to see what this reveals in pure shaping terms. Although in subsequent chapters I will place the same processes within their cultural and chronological contexts, and at the same time examine them in greater detail, there is something important to be gained by examining them stripped of their background. The way in which each process relates to the specific nature of the material can be discussed with special reference to their original development as inventive responses to this material. The types of objects produced as a result and the use to which these were put by society are entirely secondary to the invention/evolution/creation of the process. None of these processes were obvious or easy to bring into being. They all represent major shifts of attitude and much refinement and experiment on the part of their originators, most of whom are destined to remain obscure. This does not mean that their achievements cannot be celebrated for being the examples of human ingenuity they are. A history of glass is not a smooth, linear progression: processes invented over three thousand years ago have been supplanted but rarely superseded. In many cases it is impossible to even reproduce equivalents of ancient processes let alone improve on them.

This then is a review of the main glass forming processes with special reference to the unique way in which each emerges from, and is embedded in, the special nature of the material.

Although I have presented these in terms of their occurrence rather than chronologically there exists a major distinction that must be drawn between craft processes based on, and driven by, physical skills and rationalised machine processes. I have kept references to this split to a minimum, preferring to explore these differences within contextual chapters later. I have tried to keep this review to a consideration of basic material and process principles.

There is a distinction between primary and secondary methods. Primary methods engage directly with molten glass and proceed from there to the forming of a finished item; a secondary method is one that starts with intermediate glass solids and forms them by re-heating.

PRIMARY METHODS

INFLATION

Based on the fact that glass can be inflated to create a bubble (see top right), this method exploits the fact that liquid glass gradually hardens as it loses heat (and can be softened by re-heating). It is based on the controlled expansion of the bubble of glass by manipulation and the addition of further glass. Skilled repetitive movements are used to keep the form stable during forming stages.

These primarily involve constant rotation to prevent the soft glass from distorting. These hand and body movements are, once mastered, largely instinctive and form the basis of the skill of glass blowing (see bottom right). Many of the mechanised glass processes that have been invented over the past one hundred and fifty years have taken as their model this hand driven process and are, despite their automated nature, rationalisations of it (see opposite page, left column).

STATIC PRESSING

Although this process also exploits the same basic relationship between cooling hot glass and an exterior skin, it utilises compression rather than inflation. It is based on the squeezing effect on a mass of hot glass caught between two surfaces. These are usually metal and operate at a lower temperature than the glass and, therefore, draw heat from it, thereby encouraging the development of a stable, surface skin. After the initial action of the press, which brings the glass into contact with base and plunger, the forming process is static: the press mould remains a closed system until the glass is rigid enough to be released. A pressing system can be extremely basic and operated by hand pressure, as in the shaping of a simple prunt, (see opposite page, right column, and p.14) or complex as in the case of

(PREVIOUS PAGE)

(TOP) *The basic premise of glassforming by inflation. The contrast between surface skin and fluid interior makes it possible to create and expand a bubble of glass.*

(BOTTOM) *The physical nature of the craft of glassblowing. Using a wide range of extensions to the human body (blowing iron, shears, etc.) in conjunction with bodily movements the basic bubble is inflated, extended, added to and shaped.*

Photo, Janet Elliott.

(LEFT) *A basic hand procedure. The molten gather of glass is rotated into a wooden shaper to form an evenly distributed, symmetrical form prior to further blowing.*

Photo, Janet Elliott.

(BELOW LEFT) *A mechanised version of the same procedure using a power source to handle a much larger amount of glass than is possible by hand.*

Schott Glass, Germany.

(BELOW RIGHT) *Three simple, hand-held pressing tools. These were produced to allow glassmakers to impress patterns, devices, dates or names on to blobs of hot glass. They comprise two sizes of 'raspberry' and a wheatsheaf design.*

Janet Elliott. Photo, David Jones.

(ABOVE) *A group of small pressed items, two buttons and two buckles, produced in the early 19th century. Made in black glass they were intended to simulate jet which was a popular material for jewellery. Production was within factories, where workers heated rods of glass and pressed them into metal dies by the use of hand-operated fly presses. Alternatively, in Bohemia, workers pressed the items within their own cottages, using bellows-operated charcoal braziers and hand-held pincers which allowed them to squeeze the hot ductile glass between the forming dies. Much of the technology was borrowed from small-scale metalwork.*

Birmingham Museum and Art Gallery.

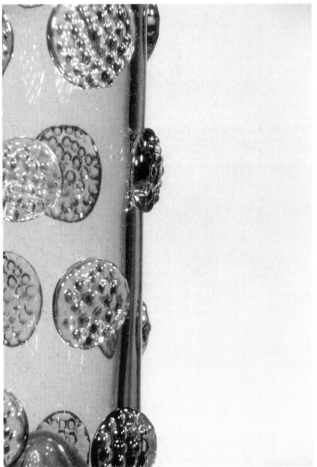

(LEFT) *The principle of press moulding as part of the physical repertoire of glassblowing. A small application of hot glass is impressed with a simple hand-held tool. This technique, unlike mechanised versions, can be easily adapted to yield a wide variety of results, from rows of prunts, as in this example, to individually impressed seals.*

Photo, Janet Elliott.

a detailed three dimensional object formed under hydraulic pressure requiring an elaborate multi-sectioned metal mould (see left and below).

(LEFT) *A simple, mechanically operated press-mould that displays the basic process. The glass object is formed through the combined action of mould and plunger on a precise amount of hot glass. The glass solidifies as it loses heat through contact with the metal mould, which is kept at a lower temperature than the glass.*

Broadfield House Glass Museum.

(BELOW) *A group of pressed glass items from the early 20th century. The use of multi-sectioned moulds allowed the production of complex objects that exploited the technology and engineering skill available. The yacht has open sections dividing its sails, which would have entailed two parts of the mould meeting to prevent the glass from entering. The mermaid soap dish has had the mould joins drawn in, to illustrate the number of sections that had to come together to form the dish, and just as importantly, break apart to release the object. This action would be repeated thousands of times a day.*

Photo, David Jones.

MOBILE PRESSING

Although this group is really a sub-section of pressing it involves mobile rather than static glass masses. The temperature of the glass is higher and the glass more liquid, and the processes use the fluid movement of the material as an essential partner in the shaping of the end products. This category includes figured sheet glass, where a stream of liquid glass is passed underneath, or between, metal patterned rollers (see opposite), which flatten and impress its surface. This exploits a variation of the relationship between mobile, elastic mass and the more rigid skin, and allows the glass to move under or between the rollers, while at the same time accepting a pattern and standard thickness. These two qualities are, of course, in contrast, and the equation between them was an obstacle that had to be overcome by the pioneers of the process. A more sophisticated variant of it is the float-glass process (see below), which is only capable of producing a flat, unpatterned sheet, where the glass mass is shaped and polished during its movement across a bed of molten tin.

(ABOVE) *Mobile pressing. The manufacture of sheet glass from a continuous stream of molten glass. Glass from the furnace is poured between rollers and drawn off in a single ribbon.*

(PREVIOUS PAGE) *The revolutionary float process developed by Pilkington in 1959. This entirely new system operates by a radical use of the liquidity of glass. The molten material is floated on a bed of molten tin to create a polished, even sheet drawn from massive tank furnaces. As with all such novel ideas, it swiftly eclipsed traditional methods of flat glass manufacture.*
Both photos Pilkington Bros Ltd Archive.

(TOP AND ABOVE) *The Danner process that continuously draws off tubing from a tank of molten glass through a ceramic shaper. Such processes rely on a partnership between the age-old properties and behaviour of glass, and the absolute control and predictability of modern technology. This contrast is brought out in the two images here. The first shows the actual shape of the hollow tube being formed, and the second the huge surrounding machine which houses the range of controls and mechanisms that precisely govern movement and temperature. Variations of these controls allow the production of different diameters of tube at the rate of up to 4 m per second.*
Top: Schott Glass, Germany. Above: British Glass Manufacturers' Federation.

MOBILE STRETCHING

The creation of sheet, rod, tube and fibre based on the stretching of a given shape. This initial shape is created by variants of a single concept, the utilisation of the inherent stickiness of hot liquid glass to adhere to a mandrel of some kind (see previous page and right).

This configuration creates a starter shape, which is stretched to elongate it and allow lengths of the product to be drawn off the mass of glass. The

(RIGHT) *The Lubbers cylinder machine. The cylinder of glass is drawn from the molten glass by a metal disk. The cylinder shape is kept constant by compressed air blown down the pipe attached to the disk. In many ways this system was a rationalisation of the action of a glassblower working the glass with his hands and lungs. However, by using this system a single cylinder of glass nearly 14.4 m in length and 60 cm in diameter could be made. Cylinders made by even the most skilled blowers could not exceed 1.80 x 0.35 m. Machines like this required the co-ordination of power sources such as gas and electricity, together with the use of compressed air and temperature controls.*

(BELOW) *The production of fine glass filaments (fibres) is achieved by drawing off sticky threads of hot glass through a perforated platinum plate, and pulling them at a precise rate directly onto spools. The relationship that exists between the surface skin and glass mass at these tiny diameters results in flexible threads that are also immensely strong.*
Both photographs, Pilkington Bros Ltd Archive.

Hot glass is deposited into a mould ready for spinning. In addition to the contours of the mould, the glass will be constrained by pegs that will interrupt the flow of glass.

Photo, Stuart Garfoot.

The spinning mould, showing the movement and shape adopted by the soft glass.

Photo, Stuart Garfoot.

Two pieces from the 'Perfora' range of centrifuged containers designed by Stuart Garfoot for Rosenthal. Based on principles developed from the experimental mould system is shown in the two top pictures; the dishes and bowls derive their unique forms from the designed interplay between the forces involved.

Courtesy Stuart Garfoot.

stretching can be achieved vertically, horizontal, or in the case of glass fibres, downwards (see p.7 and the lower picture of p.19).

All of these procedures exploit two aspects of hot glass, stickiness and elasticity.

CENTRIFUGAL FORCE

The creation of hollow forms by centrifugal pressure on a liquid mass of glass (see previous page). The process is made possible by the way in which liquid glass changes from liquid to solid states gradually as it loses heat. A given amount of glass is placed in a mould which is then rotated at speeds of up to 3000 r.p.m. The centrifugal forces push the liquid glass upwards and outwards to take up the shape and texture of the metal mould. Its precise configuration is determined by the relationship that exists between the viscosity of the glass, (dependent on its heat), the configuration of the mould and the

speed of the centrifuge. The glass gradually stops moving as it cools and solidifies. As it is a liquid while it is mobile the glass flows into the surface variations of the mould's shape.

The resultant rim shape reflects this interaction. It is a particularly 'glassy' process, and the design of the end product is dependent on the prediction and control of the way in which the glass behaves.

PRIMARY CASTING

All glass casting utilises the liquid nature of hot glass and its reaction to gravity, that is to say its pourability. At the same time all attempts to cast glass are limited by the presence of its surface skin and the way in which it hampers this movement by slowing it down and increasing its resistance. Primary casting involves the filling of a mould, which takes the form of the desired shape, and pouring liquid glass directly into it (see below and overleaf).

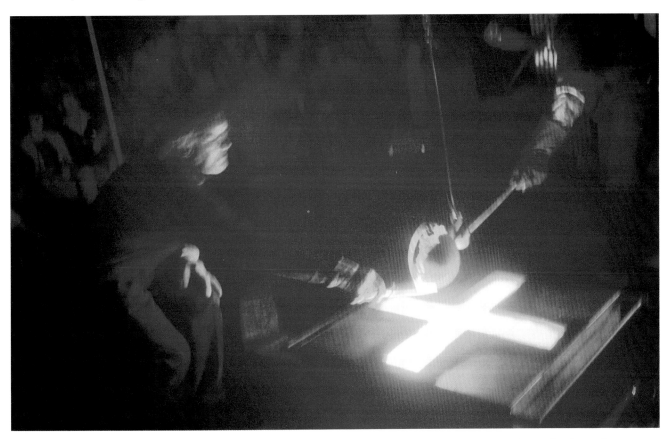

The artist and designer Bertil Vallien organising the direct hot glass casting of one of his sculptures. The forms of such casts have to follow the way in which sand casting works. An original is pushed into the sand and removed to create a void and the hot glass is poured in directly from the furnace via a ladle.
Courtesy Bertil Vallien.

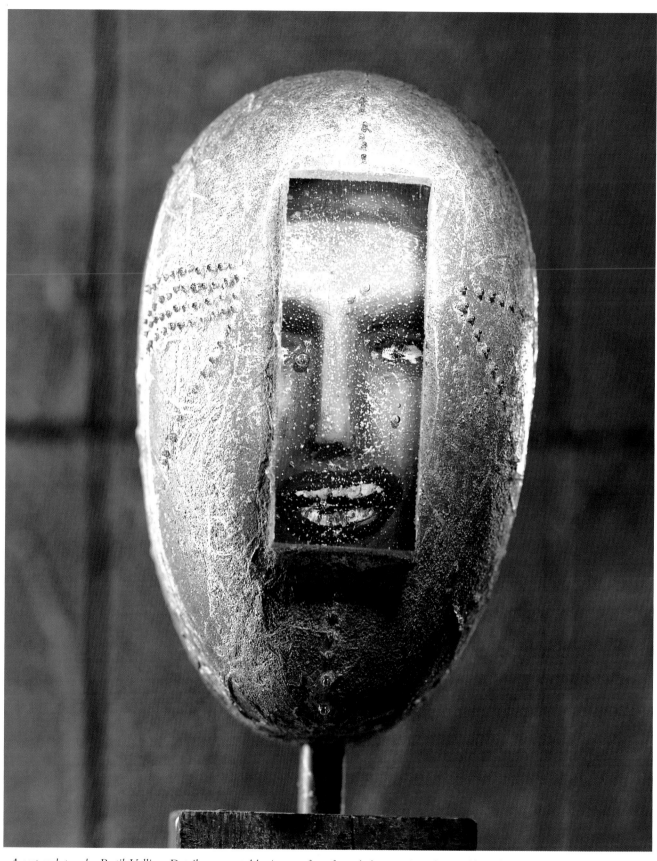

A cast sculpture by Bertil Vallien. Details are created by inserts of pre-formed glass put into the mould, and an area of polished glass allows visual access to the interior. The rest of the surface is left in its sand-cast condition.
Courtesy Bertil Vallien.

A piece by John Lewis.

Courtesy John Lewis.

This can be achieved by a variety of means depending on the size and shape of the mould. The whole casting procedure can vary from simple to highly complex: from glass gathered on an iron or in a ladle, to the use of specially designed pouring devices like tipping crucibles, which can themselves vary from tiny to huge (see left).

The American designer/maker John Lewis has developed a specialised casting furnace which can be moved and tapped to provide a stream of high quality glass for large-scale casting (see above right and below).

A crucible of optical glass being poured into a mould.

Schott Glass, Germany.

The sophistication of John Lewis's overhead casting facility. Capable of melting up to 274 kg of high quality hot glass and delivering it as a fine stream directly into moulds.

Courtesy John Lewis.

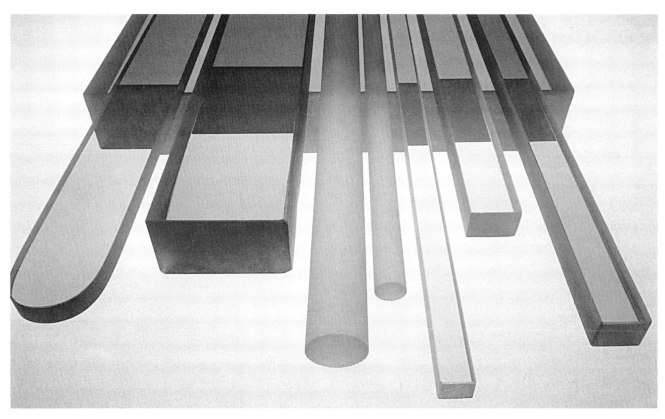

An example of a secondary glass solid. Available in a wide range of forms and colours for re-heating and forming. Such activities only require small specific heat sources such as gas/air burners or kilns.
Schott Glass, Germany.

The more mobile the mass of glass during its founding the clearer it will appear. This is why optical glass is constantly stirred, and why some factories producing high-grade lead crystal fill moulds from a stream of glass that runs constantly from their furnaces. The reason why constant mobility improves the optical qualities of the glass is, once again, a result of the interaction between the skin and the inside mass of molten glass. By constantly disturbing this mass the surface skin is folded back into the interior. Where all areas of the glass are mobile, the same conditions pertain throughout the glass, both of these activities avoid problems like striations which, not only mar its appearance but also have the potential to create stress in the final, solid state. These are caused by slight differences in the glass due to unequal founding conditions. All of the processes described so far take as their starting point glass as a hot liquid even though they all exploit slightly different aspects of it. It is perhaps worth stressing at this stage that each process, and even each slight variation of it, was often a result of many years of development and refinement before viable, repeatable versions emerged. This happened in two main ways: as evolved, empirical craft procedures like glassblowing

that emerged over time, or as single, product driven, industrial processes masterminded by individuals or small groups. A single problem within such a system could sometimes resist solution for years.

SECONDARY METHODS

The next group of processes is, in relation to glass as a hot liquid, secondary in that their starting point is glass as a solid, which is re-heated to shape it (see above).

This does not seem at first glance to constitute a radically different approach, but it is. In secondary processes (in the sense that glass has been formed hot in order to create the solid), a choice can be made about what forms of solid are selected and to what temperature (viscosity level) they are heated. These secondary solids are many: sheet, tube, rod, ingot, marbles, grain and powder. This variety not only makes it easier to form through the associated processes that depend on them, but their choice and disposition profoundly affect their end products. Often the processes and products can be seen to have derived directly from them, and would be unthinkable without them.

Beads made by the contemporary artist Kate Drew-Wilkinson. Beads were amongst the earliest glass artefacts, and are still made by heat forming and manual manipulation.

Broadfield House Glass Museum.

The fact that these processes work by the re-heating of pre-shaped glass pieces mean that the makers who use them are, therefore, independent of the glass founding process. They do not require founding furnaces or knowledge of how to make glass from basic, raw constituents. The heat sources required for secondary processes are simpler and operate at a lower temperature than those used to found glass. This fact has made a major contribution to the nature of glassforming, creating a natural division between primary and secondary workers, which often manifested itself in the form of glass workshops operating at great distances from sources of pre-shaped glass.

(TOP) *The highly directed skills of lampworking. The artist Paul Stankard working on a complex detail.*
(MIDDLE) *Using pre-formed solids, usually rods.*
(ABOVE) *Many details are encased in clear glass. The final result displays the amazing quality and precision possible.*

Courtesy Paul Stankard.

LAMP WORKING

This involves the re-heating, shaping and manipulation of glass-rods and tubes. It requires manual dexterity and skill of a high order but in a way that is different to the skills of a blower. In lamp working the shaping is more focused and dependent on the fingers and hands rather than the whole body (see right, top picture). The heat source is small and intense and in it

parts of the rod or tube can be heated to softened or semi-liquid state in a few seconds (see above, middle picture). Different rods or tubes can be joined, twisted and formed by their interaction or with a variety of tools to create an enormous variety of shapes and effects, albeit on a small scale (see above, bottom picture). It is one of the oldest glassforming techniques used originally during the Mesopotamian era to make beads. It is one of the few glass processes to have been practised continuously throughout the history of glass, perhaps because of its simple technical requirements. It is still extremely popular today.

CORE-FORMING

A process with a number of variants that is related to lampworking, particularly bead making (see right) but which derives in the first case from faience manufacture. It is exclusive to the Ancient World, originating in Mesopotamia and reaching its peak in New-Kingdom Egypt. It involves coating a friable

(RIGHT) A diagram demonstrating the relationship between beadmaking and core-forming in the Ancient World. This research, by Dudley F. Giberson, establishes the likely pre-eminence of re-heating techniques as the principal core-forming method.

Courtesy Dudley F. Giberson Jr.

To make beads use a wire mandrel, 2-3 mm thick and cover with "separator" (9 parts silica and 1 part kaolin). Here are six beads attached in black glass.

Here is a larger mandrel wire, 8-10 mm thick for making core vessels. The mandrel is covered with core material (12 parts silica to 1 part kaolin) which provides the internal shape of the vessel. Covering the core in black outline is one core-vessel with handles.

Basically there is little difference between bead making and core vessel making. *__IT IS ESSENTIALLY THE SAME TECHNOLOGY__* with the only major difference residing in scale and how the glass is applied to the mandrel/core form.

Group of core-formed vessels. They display the characteristics of artefacts made by this method. They are small in scale, opaque, richly coloured and decorated with a variety of horizontal combing techniques.
Bristol Museums and Art Gallery.

(ABOVE AND DETAIL RIGHT) *A fused bowl made from hundreds of separate cane sections. Not only can the individual circular rod sections be seen, but also the characteristic way in which these deform evenly to create an overall hexagonal pattern. Venice and Murano Glass Co. 1885.*

Broadfield House Glass Museum.

core with a homogenous layer of glass. The core is removed when cold, creating a small container form. There are at least three possible versions of this process which all suggest different ways of coating the core with a layer of glass. Once achieved the glass surface is usually decorated with horizontal bands of rod patterns distorted into complex festooning (see previous page, lower illustration).

Despite the magnificent objects that were made by core-forming it does not appear to be a logical or efficient way of shaping glass. It is an excellent illustration of Professor Hoyle's concept quoted at the beginning of this chapter, for it can only surely be understood in terms of its antecedents, beadmaking and faience. It is limited in scale and its products are extremely contaminated on their inside surfaces through contact with the core.

FUSING

The fact that, when heated, pieces of glass soften, gradually becoming sticky without losing their basic form, makes it possible to join them together while retaining the pattern created by the individual solids (see both pictures above). The fact that such solids exist in a variety of forms, such as rods, grains, strips

offers a vocabulary of possibilities. Fusing exploits both the skin surface and the distinct stages of viscosity that the material passes through on its journey from solid to liquid when heated. In such amalgams each glass piece can still be seen visually within the body of the object even though it has, through fusion, lost its structural identity. This visual definition has been used in a number of different guises since Ancient Egyptian times and can be used to yield highly complex, internal patterning, especially when differently coloured glass pieces are used (see this and following pages).

The fused, banded bowls from Alexandria produced in the third century BC and the millefiore paperweights of eighteenth century France are both

(TOP LEFT) *A group of cut* millefiore *showing the way in which paperweights are produced. The canes, made by bundling and stretching, are organised in sections within a metal ring. This is heated to prevent cracking, and covered in hot glass. It is picked up on a punty iron and the surface of the clear glass is shaped. The magnification created by this layer turns the* millefiore *canes into magical versions of their original selves. This use of two manifestations of the same material is a classic example of the versatility of glass, utilising it in such a way that the final result is much more than a mere sum of its parts.*

(ABOVE) *Two 1st century* AD *fused vessels made in Alexandria for the luxury Roman market. The rich results of this process, which grew out of the Egyptian mastery of complex cane fusions, continues to fascinate. It is still used by individual designer/makers to produce high-quality decorative artefacts. The rods follow the spiral and sunburst pattern made by folding and manipulating contrasting colours (see p.29).*
Both pictures, trustees of the Victoria and Albert Museum, London. Photos, Daniel McGrath.

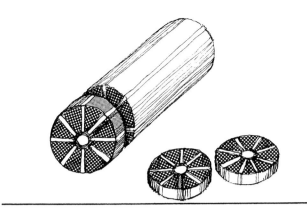

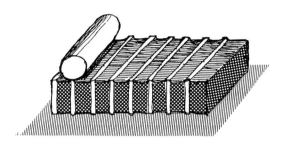

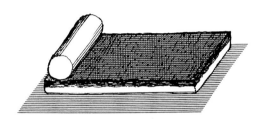

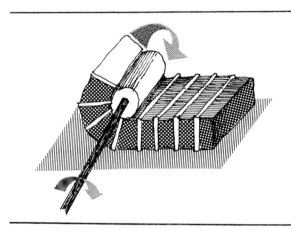

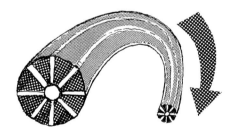

The basic flat sections of fused glass that are a feature of Egyptian glass-workshop sites were the starting points for many patterns. In this case, alternate layers of colour are picked up by a central section to create the star-shape section that is commonly found in cane-formed ware.

Author's diagram after Dr S. Dawes.

The manufacture of the common spiral section rods was, like many cross-sections, a technique involving the heating and manipulation of simple flat sections of colour. The spiral was created by folding two contrasting layers on to a central glass core that became part of the pattern. The various elements were made soft and sticky by heating in a small muffle furnace and, once put together, pulled and elongated to create lengths of rod with the miniaturised spiral running through it. This could be cut into small sections to create the individual slices required for cane fused items. The technique is the same as that used by confectioners to create seaside rock.

Author's diagram after Dr S. Dawes.

examples of the range and adaptability of this method of forming glass.

BENDING

This process exploits the intermediate softening stage between liquid and solid, when pre-shaped glass will soften and lose rigidity without any flow of material within it. This means that, within strict limits, glass can be reshaped without any distortion of the basic section (see below).

This method of forming was developed by the Syrians in the fourth century BC to shape flat discs into hollow bowls. It is still in use, particularly to shape sheet glass into three-dimensional sections for architectural use (see opposite page, lower picture). It involves heating an existing glass solid, in this case flat sheet over or into a mould which shapes the glass as it softens (see opposite page, top picture).

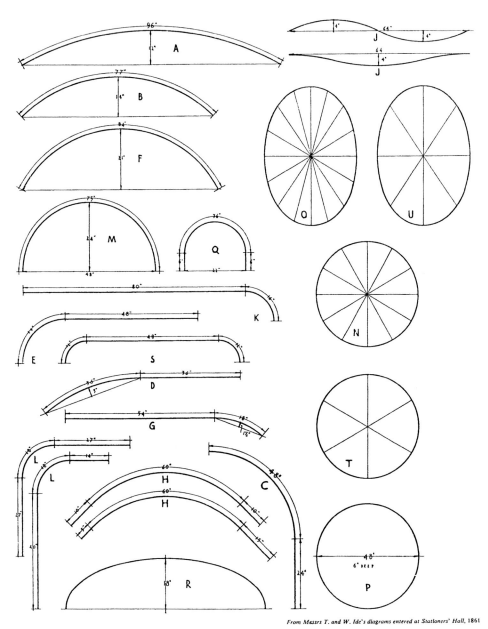

From Messrs T. and W. Ide's diagrams entered at Stationers' Hall, 1861

Fig. LXII   **Messrs T. and W. Ide's diagrams of standard bending curves**

Diagram by T.W. Ide Ltd, showing the range of bending curves possible with sheet glass. These are determined by the limitations of sheet glass as it softens and bends over convex, or into concave, moulds within architectural-scale kilns.

Photo, T.W. Ide, London.

(LEFT) *The production of architectural-scale bent glass. The steel mould has provided the forming template for a sheet of glass, under heat, within this enormous kiln. The glass has slumped under its own weight to take up the curve of the mould. Photograph from the 1930s.*

Photo, Pilkington Bros Ltd Archive.

(BELOW) *An architectural feature using bent and textured glass sheets. The installation by Warren Langley for Ozone glass involves the use of standard sheet glass that has been customised by heat forming.*

Warren Langley, Ozone Glass. Design, Tony Masters.

SECONDARY CASTING

This combines elements of primary casting and fusing. It involves shaping heated glass within a refractory mould and is the nearest equivalent in glass's forming repertoire to fine metal casting, i.e. the production of one-off items which are totally shaped by the contours and surface texture of the mould (see below). However, given the unique nature of glass there are a number of crucial differences between it and liquid metal as a castable material. These differences give rise, in turn, to the wide range of specific glass casting procedures. These stem from the turgidity of liquid glass and its resistance to flow, which makes it impossible to fill any but the simplest mould by pouring. Any complexity of form or texture means that glass has to be introduced into the mould, initially in a solid form, which can be achieved in a variety of ways, and by using the range of glass solids available from single ingots to fine dust and all the possibilities in between. The use of one glass solid form rather than another will profoundly affect the quality of the cast: fine grains, for instance, result in a translucent waxy result. Although glass has, in effect, been cast for most of its existence, a full range of complex casting procedures has only been fully developed during the last century and a half. This is closely related to its use as an expressive, sculptural process by individuals like Frederick Carder and François Décorchment (see opposite).

(ABOVE) *An example of secondary casting by Colin Reid. Moulds containing blocks of glass are placed in the kiln. When fired, the glass softens and takes up the form of the mould. Secondary casting allows the use of a variety of forms of glass solid, all of which cast with particular qualities. As a result, the range of qualities is different to, and wider than, primary casting with hot glass.*
Courtesy Colin Reid.

(OPPOSITE PAGE) *A pate-de-verre vase by F. Décorchement, 1912. The control achieved by Décorchement through his use of refractory moulds, filling, and casting systems was considerable. It is demonstrated within this unique object where it has enabled him to cast the scarab details accurately in a different colour glass to the main body of the vase.*
Musée des Arts Decoratifs, Paris. Photo, L. Sully-Jaulme.

(LEFT) *Stages in the process of kiln casting. The production of the original form in wood is followed by a rubber mould, which enables the form to be reproduced in wax. The wax is embedded in a castable refractory and then steamed out to create a void into which crushed glass can be kiln fused. This process, which is derived from metal casting, is called lost-wax casting.*

(BELOW) *A cast piece by Colin Reid. The glass used to fill the mould was a pre-formed block of optical glass. The resulting cast has picked up the textures of the mould, yet retains the pure, optical quality of the original block. Selective polishing has revealed this.*

Both courtesy Colin Reid.

The destruction of the mould each time an object is produced has meant that casting is unsuited to series production, and its post-industrial development has been by, and for, individuals as an artistic process by which to manipulate their chosen medium, glass (see previous page).

Because of this, wide variations of the basic process have evolved, often closely bound up with the nature of each practitioner's artistic vision. Such variations are also related to the choice of glass solids used to fill the mould and the impact this choice has on the formal vocabulary of the resulting glass mass and surface. The smaller the particles, the less liquid the glass will become during casting and the less the final cast will conform to traditional glass stereo-types. As previously stated this choice can vary widely from single pre-cast pieces to thousands of tiny fragments. Each piece of glass, no matter how large or small, will create its own skin round it as it is heated. If one single ingot is used (only possible within simple, open moulds), there is a correspondingly small amount of skin area to contaminate the transparency of the glass and as a result this method produces the most visually pure casts. In contrast, a mould filled with a number of separate pieces will result in a cast which is marked internally with the junctions these pieces make as their surfaces fuse together. This is, of course, for some artists the main reason for choosing to cast glass this way, as it offers particular qualities of internal pattern and light manipulation within the body of the glass. Because grains of glass, even when subjected to high temperatures, tend to coagulate in a mass rather then flow, a number of highly specific casting techniques have evolved to counter this characteristic and harness the qualities that fine-grain casting give. Many of these techniques have been hidden behind the mystique created round the artists who used them, sometimes deliberately. Two techniques have suffered in this way and perhaps need to be described in some detail.

Pâte-de-verre A Generic term which emerged in France during the second half of the nineteenth century (probably coined by Henri Cros) to describe a basic method of multi-coloured glass casting using finely crushed glass grains and powders. At its simplest the crushed glass was carefully placed in the mould to disperse the various colours into the details. The mould was cast from a mixture of materials including plaster and powdered refractories. The whole was heated to a temperature at which the individual glass grains would fuse. On cooling the mould would be broken away and the glass cast cleaned and polished. The great advantage of this method is that unlike other glass processes it can place colour precisely into areas of detail, in fact its great pioneer Henri Cros specifically began his experiments in order to achieve a polychrome sculptured process. He was hampered by the relatively small scale range of glass casting in relation to true sculptural needs. His basic process was taken up by a number of other artists who refined and customised it for their own use. Two of them, Amalric Walter and Argy Rousseau attempted the series manufacture of *pâte-de-verre* casts by standardising mould making and filling, and as a result there are many of their designs in existence. However, the main barrier to mass production, which they never really addressed or solved, is the fact that each mould is destroyed in the creation of a single cast. It was, and remains a specialist fine art process in the sense that it is suited to the production of high value single items. It is interesting to note that the unique tiles of glass/ceramic amalgam that cover the American space shuttle and provide its heat shield are cast in this way.

Cire perdue The production of a mould which contains a void in the shape of the glass form to be cast is probably the most difficult aspect of casting. It is usually achieved by casting the mould around a wax model, which is melted out to create the void. This part of the process is called *cire perdue* or 'lost wax', and is not a specifically glass associated process having been developed originally for metal casting. Its use in relation to glass often results in confusion and provides a convenient label to place on glass objects whose manufacture origins are unknown, as a result it is often misapplied. Far more René Lalique items are described as being made by *cire perdue* than is borne out by close examination, for example.

This review of the main glass forming processes is only intended to provide an indication of the ways in which the range of processes relate

Containers at Baccarat filled with a mix of cullet, batch and red lead prior to being emptied into furnaces to produce full lead crystal. Archives Baccarat. Photo, Jacques Boulay.

closely to and exploit the peculiar qualities of glass, each process depending on an individual relationship with it. Each process's development will be dealt with in detail during the historical survey and they are, in any case, far from fixed – for they are subject to seemingly endless variations and modifications, particularly within our own post-industrial era. As Douglas and Frank say 'Corning Glass at one time said that 70% of their current products had not been in production 10 years previously. This exemplifies dramatically the possibilities of finding new uses for glasses, sometimes new outlets for traditional glasses and sometimes the production of new glasses with specific properties.'[4]

Many of these specialist products stem from the sheer variability of the material governed by an increasing knowledge of, and control over, its synthetic nature. The fact that glass is a solution rather than a compound, means that its ingredients can be varied over a wide range, as can the proportions of those ingredients – each variation yielding a different kind of glass possessing different properties. Prior to our own era these variations occurred in two main ways: accident or experiment. An example of the former being the substitution of bracken for barilla as the source of flux when trade routes disappeared with the break-up of the Roman Empire, and an example of the latter being the use of large quantities of red lead by Ravenscoft in his search for a glass to rival Venetian crystal (see opposite). Although both of these changes had a profound effect on the nature of the glass produced, resulting in Waldglas and English lead crystal respectively, neither process was under the direct control or understanding of the glass makers. The majority of glass's history and development took place prior to the scientific revolution of the last two centuries that has provided a fuller understanding of the principles involved. Knowledge about the function of the constituents that go to produce glass and the optimum conditions for their interaction has substituted control and predictability for mystery and empirical ritual. This shift in approach has allowed glass to be constantly altered to serve new functions across a wide range of fields and activities, from aesthetics to engineering. With such knowledge the properties and behaviour can be virtually changed at will. As a result two surprising axioms emerge: whatever you think glass is, the opposite is also true, and glass has no *natural* characteristics, only those which are engineered synthetically by the composition and founding of the material. Two examples will suffice: flexible glass-fibres and toughened sheet are at opposite ends of the scale in terms of performance, and yet are part of the same material designation.

Many of these changes have been fuelled by the need for increased output from less input and for ever greater standardisation of products. Michael Owens's bottle-making machines and Pilkington's flat glass process being pre-eminent examples.

Although the characteristics of glass as a material can apparently be varied at will to provide artists, makers, engineers, scientists, architects and industrialists with properties appropriate to their product needs, the way in which the material behaves as a viscous liquid continues to dominate its actual shaping. The basic principles that underlie the forming procedures rely on their relationship to the mass/skin character of hot glass and to the vocabulary of physical peculiarities that stem from it: flow, stickiness and elasticity, and above all the way that these can be determined by heat levels.

CHAPTER TWO

The Technology of Glass

'Glass making, already effected by Roman times, was scarcely at all improved until the rise of modern science created a demand for specialised types of optical and resistant glass.'

Charles Singer, *The History of Technology*, 1956, vol. II.

B ecause it is a solution rather than a compound, the ingredients, their mixtures and variations that can be combined to produce a particular glass can be interpreted widely. The basis of glass is silica in the form of naturally occurring sand or from flint (ground silicous rocks) melted at a relatively high temperature (see right). The higher the silica content of the mixture the higher the temperature required to melt it and the harder the resulting glass. A normal silica content would be 50-80% with melting temperatures of around 1200°C (2192°F). The second main constituent is a flux that will lower the temperature at which the mixture will melt and form a glass. Flux can take a number of forms: soda, originally from the ash of burned aquatic plants (barilla), or potash, from the ash of woodland plants like bracken (fougiere), have been the most common throughout glass history. Both soda (sodium carbonate) and potash (potassium carbonate) are now produced chemically and are, therefore, available as identical products worldwide, but when these could only be obtained by burning specific plants their availability had a profound influence on the silica they were mixed with. Silica's natural and local characteristics not only affected the glass made from it, but also affected the direction in which the perception of glass and its use evolved. An extreme case being the impact on Venetian glass development of the silica derived from crushed flint pebbles dredged from local riverbeds. The fortuitous purity of the resulting silica allowing the production of crystal-like glass, and permanently affected glass making in Europe (see p. 39).

A molecular model of the structure of glass. A major part of the character of silica-based solutions is determined by the way its molecules become frozen in a loose configuration as it converts from liquid to solid (with a medium range glass this occurs at around 500°C). The molecules simply stop moving and do not arrange themselves into a geometric lattice as the vast majority of materials do. Its resulting open structure causes its propensity to transparency and fragility.

Science Museum Picture Library, London.

An example of Venetian crystal. Note the thinness of the overall form and the care taken to avoid a build up of glass mass, particularly in the hollow stem. This was in response to its general lack of light-refracting qualities. Its reputation as a 'crystal' glass was, in the 16th century, based on its clarity in comparison with other contemporary glasses.
Photo, Derek Balmer.

Potash glass. Developed in central/northern areas of Europe in the 17th century as control increased over the glassmaking process, particularly in the purification of glass's constituent materials and the role of added trace elements. The result was a pure refractive glass that lent itself to cutting and engraving.

Photo, Derek Balmer.

'Ocular' range of drinking glasses designed for Rosenthal by Stuart Garfoot. A major feature of this handmade range is the use of the application of hot glass – the prunt – that softens the main body of the vessel and creates a visual and actual distortion. In technique and spirit it shares much with the medieval thumbprint beaker. (See p.42)
Courtesy Stuart Garfoot.

The breakdown of trade routes during the Dark Ages cut European glass makers off from imported sources of soda ash, and forced them to adapt to the use of the radically different local potash. Generally speaking, soda-rich glasses are hard and only moderately refractive while potash-rich glasses are softer and correspondingly bright. This enforced use of local potash had a major influence on the development of European glass (see previous page, above and p.42). The particular properties of Waldglas and Bohemian crystal both relied on it for their different aesthetic qualities.

The third major glass ingredient is a stabiliser to prevent the synthesis from breaking down into its components, literally 'de-vitrifying'. The simplest form of stabiliser is lime, derived from limestone. The basic glass mix is simple and capable of enormous variations, both accidental and deliberate. It will also tolerate the presence of a range of contaminants without preventing the formation of a glass when heated. However, the presence of a naturally present contaminant or a deliberately added extra ingredient can also profoundly affect the qualities of the glass. The accidental presence of iron produces a beautiful lustrous green or blue tint to the glass, whereas the experimental addition of red lead in the seventeenth century resulted in lead crystal. Each variation in the batch constituents and its founding conditions can affect the quality, durability, working characteristics or aesthetic appearance of the material. Yet despite the simplicity of the basic pre-industrial glass mixture it must have required a lengthy process of experiment, adaptation, tacit knowledge, luck and accident to develop it in the first place. Its survival relied on hands-on empirical lines of succession. As P.T. Nicholson remarks of ancient glass workers 'Early glass makers carefully observed the results of their

Cunieform tablet – the first written account of glassmaking. The translation of these tablets in 1971 provided hard evidence of a glassmaking tradition that included Mesopotamia as a formative glass area.

(PREVIOUS PAGE)
An *example of* Waldglas. *The characteristic, and extremely beautiful, blue-green cast to this glass was the result of iron contaminants in the local ingredients that the forest glassmakers were forced to use. The break-up of the Roman Empire had cut off purer sources of potash from Alicante. That this at first unwanted colour became synonymous with objects made with it is demonstrated by the fact that even after access to Spanish barilla was restored in the 17th century, iron was deliberately added to the mixture. A classic example of a successful use of initially unwelcome qualities.*

work…how many of the trace elements were recognised and added deliberately is doubtful e.g. antimony or manganese ore were present in identified sources e.g. sand'[5]. Repeatability often codified into magic or ritual allowed predictable results without fully understanding the reasons for them (see left). Strangely the flexibility of the glass batch is responsible for both its ability to be used without full scientific control over it and for the continued development of specific glasses with unique designed properties that modern glass technology makes possible. Not until the industrial revolution did glass technology begin to allow glass making to become an understood and controllable scientifically-based activity.

The overriding ingredient for the production of glass from its raw constituents is, of course, heat: to achieve this synthesis directly requires a temperature of 11–1200°C (2012–2192°F), and modern furnaces can work at 1500°C (2732°F). Yet until the 17th century furnaces could rarely reach and hold a temperature of 1000°C (1832°F). In order to melt glass without the necessary heat to fully synthesise the ingredients an intermediate stage was added. This fritting process continued to be a necessary part of glassmaking until recently in some circumstances. Fritting involved the part melting of the ingredients in shallow pans, which allowed the presentation of a large surface area to the heat source. This burned off potentially contaminating residues and created a partial and intermediate form of glass. This was pulverised and formed the basis of the batch for the actual glass melt. Even this apparently unwelcome extra stage had a benign influence on the development of glass due to the reaction to and utilisation of it by early glassmakers.

The Ancient Egyptians produced three distinct materials based on silica with varying amounts of alkali, lime and copper: these were faience, Egyptian blue and glass. These three are distinct, separate materials but they are at the same time, in physical terms, stages in a single continuous process. As P. T. Nicholson says, 'It is not unlikely that faience, blue and glass were all made in close proximity, possibly in the same workshop complex'. It is also likely, in my opinion, that the intermediate semi-glass produced during the fritting stage contributed to the development of faience and

Egyptian blue. It is certainly the only period of history when these three materials have existed together.

During its five thousand year history, continuity of a kind has been maintained within the traditions of glassmaking, despite its dramatic shifts of formal emphasis. In the absence of a written, scientific account of the principles behind its manufacture, its survival and development have been ensured through physical and practical means based on the skills required to shape it. The history of glass until well into the 19th century was characterised by the movement of skilled workers from established centres who carried with them the full range of accumulated knowledge required to set up new ones. The well documented attempts by the Venetian authorities to protect its virtual monopoly during its heyday by preventing such migration is evidence enough, but many other examples exist. The Huguenot names in the graveyards of Stourbridge in England (Henzell and Tyzack) and the poaching of English glassmakers to Steuben and Tiffany are further examples of the importance of information and skills residing within living individuals rather than within abstract volumes. Attempts were made from earliest times to establish written repositories of glassmaking knowledge from the cunieform tablets of 7th century BC to the writings of Theophilus, Neri and the Encylopaedists. The attempts were, however, only ever partially successful because such works could not contain truly scientific principles prior to our own era, or adequately present a purely physical set of skills.

Because of the rigid social division between artisan and academic, particularly in the West, the people who wrote about glassmaking were not makers in any true sense of the word. Their accounts were primarily observed descriptions rather than records based on practical experience. The results were, to borrow a phrase from Ada Polak, able only 'to inform rather than instruct'.[6] It was not until the work and writings of individuals like Neri, Merret and Kunckel that theory and practice existed within the same person. Even then, such writings were about technology – making glass as a material rather than shaping it through craft skill. The glass blower, who, when asked how long it took him to blow a goblet replied 'twenty years and twenty minutes' was emphasising the nature of his craft knowledge as a cumulative, physical activity. Technologically, the history of glass has been for much of its history, a basically simple process handed from one generation to the next, codified within a physical, aural tradition. This line of succession was often contained within families (Baroviers in Venice for over 500 years, for example). This is particularly true of the craft of glassblowing which dominated glassforming for almost two thousand years, and which was eminently suited to such a tradition. In fact its dominance was only broken by the twin influences of a documented, scientifically based technology and the industrial revolution in the 19th century. Prior to this, the essential linear tradition could be disrupted by conquest, war, politics or shifts of world trade, but never completely destroyed. New centres and working dynasties were established, but always seeded by small groups of individuals who collectively carried the necessary knowledge and skills to bridge the gap. An example being the establishment of glassmaking in America (after a number of false starts) by European *émigrés* like Amelung and Stiegel. Each such shift brought about changes, new types of glass, new processes and new objects appropriate to the new society they served, none more so than in the New World. Nevertheless, within this constantly evolving picture there are some surprisingly simple and enduring principles at work, particularly in terms of the manufacture of the material. The basic ingredients, or workable variations of them, are available across a wide area of the earth's surface. The simplest furnace required to turn these (eventually) into glass is a rudimentary structure of clay or stone fired by wood or charcoal. Not until the use of fuels like coal and oil did such simple systems give way to larger, more complex and specialised versions. These coincided with the establishment of single product factories designed to facilitate the mass production of items like bottles. In an ironic twist, the studio glass movement, begun by Harvey Littleton in America during the 1960s was predicated on the design of a basic, simple furnace that was, in many ways, the equivalent of the medieval forest furnace. Such a facility allowed glass to become a creative medium under the control of the artist within the studio.

The development of the furnace and of the glass batch ingredients and mixtures is presented as a background to the central theme of this volume, and in relation to their contribution to, and influence over, the making of glass. It is perhaps worth stressing once more that events outside the glass-makers control made at least as large a contribution to the direction and development of glass as deliberate, fair-weather decisions. The unwelcome effects of war, competition, government ethics (banning of wood as fuel) taxes, shifts of style and loss of market were often neutralised by highly inventive responses and were, therefore, beneficial in the longer term.

CHAPTER THREE

Process Development

'Artefacts do not spring fully formed from the mind of some maker, but rather become shaped
and re-shaped through the experience of their users within the social, cultural and technological
contexts in which they are embedded.'
Henry Petrowski, *The Evolution of Useful Things*, London, 1993.

'One only truly understands what one can create'.
Giambattista Vico, *The New Science*, 1774.

It is perhaps pointless to speculate about the existence of a single origin of glass as an independent material. It is, in my opinion, unlikely that it emerged fully formed as the result of a single 'Eureka' discovery. It seems much more likely that it developed gradually and, consistent with the general theme of this book, as a result of cumulative observations and adjustments by generations of glass workers. It is more fruitful to speculate about this evolution from the clues embedded within glass objects themselves and, where these do not exist, within descriptions of their manufacture. It is worth stressing two things about the Ancient World and its attitudes to and uses of glass. First its enormous time frame, three millennia, and second the fact that during the whole of this period it did not develop the primary process of glassblowing as a forming method. The reasons for this are to be found within the material, the technological context within which glass developed and, perhaps above all, the cultural context, which established the aesthetic and economic value systems that determined its direction.

Glass probably owes its existence to an interaction between the established systems for working ceramic and metal, and the lapidary carving of semi-precious stones. The glazing of quartz pebbles in the Pre-Dynastic era, 3000 BC established a number of important starting points for the evolution of glassforming, which were to influence the course of its development profoundly. Egyptian faience production and the glazing of pebbles both work from the idea of a layer of glass existing, and being given shape by an inner core of another material. In fact faience, despite its strong individual identity, is like glass, made from crushed quartz or sand and mixed with small amounts of lime and soda ash. It almost certainly existed before glass and, therefore, helped to create the circumstances for its evolution. All that is required to turn a basic faience mixture into genuine glass is a greater amount of alkali and more/longer heating. In fact, Egyptian blue, which is also of great antiquity, is a material with the same basic ingredients that sits somewhere between faience and glass and is 'part of a continuation of materials based on silica'.[7] Faience utilises a variety of techniques to create a glaze layer on a silica core. They all involve the establishment of a fused surface layer to achieve a coloured, coherent skin. This, it seems to me, is too close to the major Egyptian glass process, core-forming to be coincidental. It also suggests at least one way in which a core can be coated with a homogenous glass layer.

Hot trailing. An apparently simple procedure, where a blob of hot glass is rotated round the bubble. The sheer scale of this example and the use of contrasting colours make its use dramatic. This basic technique has been used for 2000 years, yet talented individuals still find new ways to use it. English, early 19th century. (See p.72)
Broadfield House Glass Museum. Photo, David Jones.

CORE-FORMING

The most characteristic, and basic of, ancient glass forming processes was almost certainly developed originally by the Mesopotamian civilisation that flourished in the area between the Tigris and Euphrates. It probably reached Egypt as a concept, if not as a fully-fledged process, through high level cultural exchange. This is suggested by the existence of a few surviving fragments of Mesopotamian core-formed vessels and the fact that the fully fledged Egyptian glass industry that appeared during the reign of Thutmosis III in the 15th century BC used a Mesopotamian word 'mekku' to describe glass. These original versions were however fairly basic, and core-forming was undoubtedly brought to its highest levels of technical and artistic achievement during dynastic Egypt. Looked at purely logically, core-forming does not appear to be a likely or promising way of shaping glass. It is only when its likely origins are taken into account that its existence makes sense. At its most basic it involves

the coating of a core of soft, friable material, itself established round a solid copper or bronze rod, with a coherent and continuous layer of glass. The core creates the internal form of the vessel, and is both solid enough to remain unchanged during coating with glass, and weak enough to be removed after coating. This, after cooling, creates a hollow glass vessel, albeit one which is small in scale and extensively contaminated on its interior surface by residues of the core material. The devising of such a core material must have been extremely difficult as it had to possess a number of contradictory properties, not least the need to allow the sticky glass enough surface purchase to adhere during the forming procedure, while remaining separate enough to allow easy removal on cooling. The fact that core formed vessels invariably carry the remnants of core material and texture on their interiors (unless removed by grinding and polishing) shows that the composition was a compromise solution. Much speculation has been generated concerning the precise composition of the core.

A selection of basic, intermediary glass solids available to, and used by, glass workers in the Ancient World. These were used in secondary forming techniques where such solids were softened by re-heating and manipulated into their final form using only a small heat source.
Pilkington Bros Ltd Archive.

Clay, sand, fabric, even camel dung have been suggested, and may all be contenders or have provided ingredients. The true novelty of the core undoubtedly lay in the exact composition and disposition of its ingredients. During experiments in the re-creation of core-formed vessels it was found that the hardest part of the process was the initial coating of glass on the core.[8] Once established it required great skill to keep it in position, and it became clear that the most important property of the core was its performance at its surface contact with the glass. As I have already said, it is an unlikely process until its cuckoo-like origins in glazing, faience and bead making are remembered, for without them I cannot imagine that it could have developed.

The way in which a coating of glass was put on to the core is a matter of debate and there exists a number of variants as suggested methods. In any case it seems unlikely that a process that was practised for at least a thousand years had only one manifestation, and I present three alternatives, all of which could have been used in various places and times. There may have been others but, if there were, I am convinced that they must have worked within the same parameters as these three. Before describing them in any detail it is necessary to speculate about the background to the process in terms of the forms taken by the glass and their influence on the basic process. To do this it is necessary to draw a distinction between glassmaking and glass shaping, particularly in the Ancient World. This is because the processes used during the three millennia prior to the invention of glassblowing (about the same time as the birth of Christ) took as their starting point a solid, cold form of glass, rod, ingot, grain or lump (see previous page), in contrast to processes like blowing, which only begin once glass has been produced as a hot, molten liquid. A prerequisite of glassblowing is that molten glass is founded on the same site as its shaping, a fact that led to the establishment of glass factories in Rome by the end of the 1st century AD. The system that operated in the Ancient World was predicated on the re-heating of intermediate forms of glass (see right). Shaping could be, and was, carried out independently of and separately to the founding of the original glass used to make the rods etc. There is

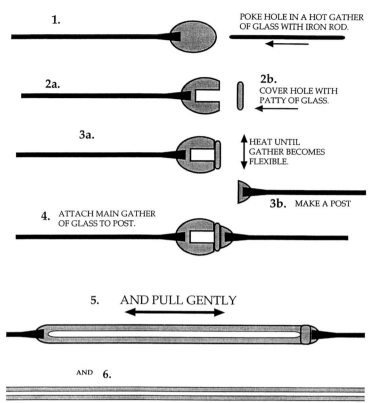

THIS IS THE ANCIENT TUBE-PULLING TECHNIQUE,
Rediscovered By Dudley Giberson In 1976
And Used Since Then To Make All Giberson Glass Tube Beads

1. POKE HOLE IN A HOT GATHER OF GLASS WITH IRON ROD.

2a.

2b. COVER HOLE WITH PATTY OF GLASS.

3a.

HEAT UNTIL GATHER BECOMES FLEXIBLE.

3b. MAKE A POST

4. ATTACH MAIN GATHER OF GLASS TO POST.

5. AND PULL GENTLY

AND 6.

Glass Tube Made Without A Blowpipe
1500 B.C. to 1995 A.D.

A diagram outlining a method of producing glass tubing by hand. This is consistent with the glass techniques available to makers prior to the development of glassblowing, and is a convincing explanation for its production in the Ancient World. It is the result of practical research by Dudley F. Giberson.

Photo, Dudley F. Giberson Jr.

much evidence to suggest that such intermediate glass forms were moved large distances around the Ancient World for final shaping within specialist workshops. The blue glass ingots formed in the Ulu Burun shipwreck, which also contained large quantities of other intermediate raw materials like sheets of copper, are perhaps the most spectacular examples.[9]

This point is of more than mere academic, historical interest, for the nature of glass as a raw material always exercises a profound effect on the way in which the forming processes themselves evolve (see p.50, top picture). All of the processes used during the various civilisations of the Ancient World derived much of their internal logic from the

49

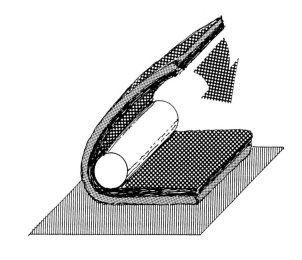

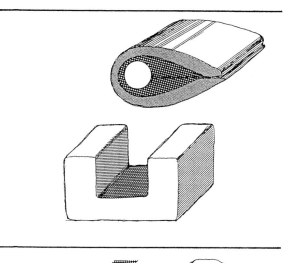

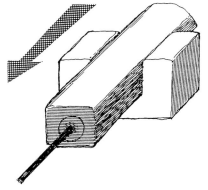

creative use of these fixed starting points that they did not make themselves, but brought in from specialist sources (see previous page, top picture). The main processes used in the pre-Christian era were: cane fusion (see right and next page), flame working, casting, slumping and, of course, core-forming. Each linked to a basic glass solid or a more sophisticated grouping of solids. This, and the fact that Egyptian glassworkers viewed glass from the same perspective as stone or metal lies at the heart of the way in which they and the Mesopotamians viewed and worked glass. For them it shared many of the characteristics of semi-precious stones, it was available in a semi-formed state and lent itself to the production of similar qualities. The fact that the Ancient World prized opaque, highly coloured glass with complex internal and surface patterning in preference to qualities like transparency may well originate from its availability and cultural context. It is worth exploring this notion of transparency in relation to Egyptian glass in particular, largely because it contrasts so sharply with our own use and perceptions. Transparency, and in particular colourless clear glass requires the use of decolourisers within the basic batch to counteract the contaminants usually encountered in the silica used. Without a full understanding of the chemistry involved, clear, colourless glass could only be achieved by access to pure materials and accidental traces of manganese (which acts as a decolouriser). It has sometimes been suggested that the Egyptian preference for glass as a predominantly opaque, highly coloured material is actually caused by their

A characteristic of cane-section amalgams is that they appear to be formed from folded layers of coloured glass, sometimes incorporating rods to create circular details. This is particularly true of the eye and the spiral section. In addition, such blocks have clearly been shaped after folding into regular, rectangular sections. This would suggest that during elongation (to miniaturise), the glass has been pulled through a rigid former. This is borne out by the horizontal markings on the sides of the blocks, which are consistent with such movement. Shaping cross-sectioned patterns like this made it easier to incorporate slices into complex patterns involving many separate details. (See pp 56 and 57)

Author, after Dr. S Dawes.

Pulling rods by hand. A mass of glass is stretched between two irons.

Plowden and Thompson Ltd (both pictures).

Great control can be exerted by skilled glassmakers over the diameter of the rods produced. This method has remained in constant use for over 2000 years.

inability to produce a consistent clear version. This may have some truth in it, but as P. T. Nicholson says of a rare example of New Kingdom clear glass, 'The fact that clear glass could be produced at such an early date…emphasises that the Egyptians did not need to colour their glass, but rather that this was a matter of choice.'

There are two important principles at work here: firstly, that throughout its history, glass technology has been largely driven by preferences, and secondly, that glass has often relied on its contextual history for these preferences. In order to fully appreciate the glass and processes of these early civilisations it is necessary to lose our contemporary prejudices about the 'true' nature of glass. It is in fact an infinitely variable synthetic material with no natural properties at all in visual or behavioural terms. The particular set of properties that glass possesses at any specific period in history is the result of an equation of forces, some under the direct control of humankind and some imposed through availability of raw materials or lack of knowledge – few, if any, are inevitable. Certainly core-forming is enhanced by the use of an opaque glass matrix, not least to mask the residue of the forming core that adheres to the internal surfaces even after its removal. In terms of the ways in which glass was established on to the core the main methods were probably as follows:

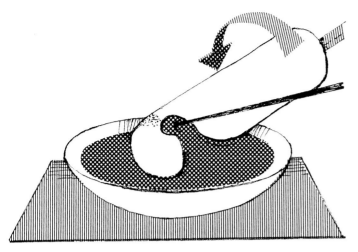

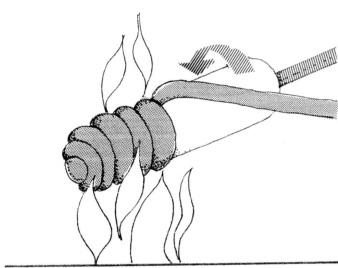

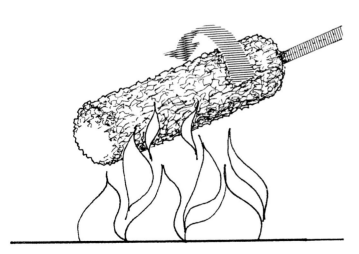

The three main suggested methods by which core-formed vessels could have been produced:
1) gathering liquid glass from a shallow dish of hot glass,
2) winding a ribbon of softened glass,
3) softening a layer of crushed glass.

1 *Hot trailing.* Suggested by Dominick Labino and demonstrated as feasible by his practical experiments. This involved shallow ceramic dishes of liquid glass (such dishes have been found by archaeologists). The core would be rotated at the surface of the glass and a metal rod would be used to pick up a trail of liquid glass and wind it on to the core. Although Labino's experiments proved this is an effective method of covering a core with glass his objects were unlike the originals in one important aspect: their surfaces are extremely glossy and even in colour, the results are more like blown objects than exact examples of Egyptian core forming. Undoubtedly such examples have become eroded during their long and eventful lives but there is a quality within their glass structure that suggests the existence of another possible variant.

2 *Ribbon winding* (see left). Based on the use of a thin rod or strip of glass, heated, softened and wound round the core. Heating was probably achieved by a bellows fed charcoal fire contained within a small ceramic muffle. The ribbon would be smoothed out by re-heating and rolling it onto a flat surface (Marvering[10]) to create a homogenous, even skin. This technique is extremely difficult in practice but does, if desired, yield a spiral pattern within the glass (see p.54, left). It follows the contemporary metal technique of tube making in which a heated metal strip was wound round a solid rod. It was undoubtedly used for some core-forming but is, in my opinion, unlikely to have been a central version of the process. It does have the advantage for the maker of only requiring a small re-heating facility like modern lampworking or flame working in the Ancient World. It is not necessary to heat any quantity of glass, except that being manipulated.

3 *The crushed glass method.* In this procedure a layer of finely crushed glass is applied to the core as a cold layer, bound on by the addition of an organic binder (egg white or honey). This is then heated by rotation in a flame (see ribbon method) to melt the grains together, and it is continuously marvered to create a homogenous skin. This method mirrors faience techniques, where cores of silica are covered with glaze, cold, prior to

An example of a ribbon-wound vessel, in this section of an alabastron from the 1st century BC. *By using a ribbon of more than one colour, the method has left its mark in the spiral pattern.*
Bristol Museums and Art Gallery.

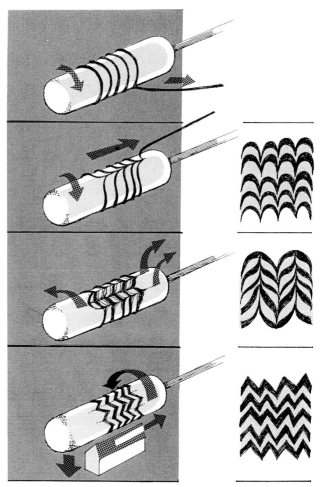

The three main methods used to create the characteristic horizontal combed and distorted decoration of core vessels.

firing. There are in existence many Egyptian core-formed items that appear to present a more granular surface than would be produced by either ribbon or trailing. There also exist a small number of asymmetric items[11] that could not have been covered by these methods and for which the crushed glass method exists as a possible procedure. In practice this is effective, requires only a small heat source and is consistent with ancient technology.

These three methods may represent some or all of the primary core-covering techniques. They do contain the main suggestions of historians, glass workers and archaeologists to date. However, once the core was covered with an effective layer of glass the next stage of detailing and decorating could take place. There is very little disagreement about how this was achieved. Details like rims and handles were formed by the addition of applied sections of hot, ductile rod, manipulated by pincers and other forming tools. The highly characteristic horizontal bands were achieved in two distinct stages. Softened canes were wound round the form on to the surface of the still warm glass. Once these bands were marvered into the soft surface layer they were distorted by a variety of methods to create the characteristic patterns. There are three distinct types of distortion (see above).

1 Single combing. A metal spike is pulled through the bands along the length of the object at regular intervals round its circumference. This gives a single distortion of the rows of colour, one which is remarkably similar to the results obtained by John Northwood's combing machine in the late 19th century. (see pp 160 and 161)

2 Double combing. Here the procedure is carried

out twice, once in each direction. This has the effect of feathering the distortion.

3 Rolled. The core, with its layer of soft glass and coloured bands in place is pushed on to a corrugated marver. This creates a more rigid zigzag pattern and is identical to the technique used in the creation of aggri beads. After the zigzag pattern has been established the surface is restored by flattening. This style of decoration is particularly evident on the cylindrical or flat-sided kohl tubes as their shape lends itself to this method.

The core-forming process was so specific to the cultural attitudes of the early civilisations that it disappeared with them. Not only was it rapidly supplanted after the development of glassblowing but it has never been subject to any kind of revival or re-assessment – in this it is unique. It is, on the face of it, not the most logical of processes unless its direct antecedents are taken into account, particularly faience and bead making with glass-rods, both of which used the principle of working on a core, quartz on the one hand, and copper wire on the other. Despite its inherent difficulties and apparent inconsistency as a glassforming process the quality and aesthetic charge of the best core-formed vessels are the equal of any made from other more obvious and better understood methods.

ROD-BASED PROCESSES AND TECHNIQUES

It is fair to say that the Egyptian glass workers exploited the potential of rod manipulation and fusion in ways that have no equal in glass history.

Even the *millefiore* and *reticelli* products of Venice in the 16th and 17th centuries are not their equals, relying as they do on glassblowing for a major part of their production.

The main individual processes within the general rod-based method can be divided into three main types with distinctly different product outcomes.

1 BEAD MANUFACTURE

This is almost certainly the oldest of rod-using processes. Its importance and wide dispersion throughout the Ancient World may well have caused the development of consistent sources of rod production and their trade in the first place. The earliest surviving beads rely on the use of a small scale, localised heat source, and the development of high levels of manipulative skill. It needs a minimum of specialised equipment and is similar to lampworking which has been carried out virtually unchanged throughout the history of glass. As with much heat centred glassmaking the only major changes have been in heat sources, fuels and the availability of more sophisticated types of glass, for example, borosilicate.

The importance and diversity of rod-based processes throughout the Ancient World was supported by an attitude to its products that is far removed from our own. Glass, for the Egyptians (and Mesopotamians before them[12]) was the equal of highly prized precious stones, with the added advantage of control over their manufacture (see below and overleaf). Items like glass beads carried none of the stigma that surrounds the use of glass in jewellery in our own era, glass was not seen as an

A magnificent example of a gold alabastron from the 1st century BC. *These small ceremonial objects relate to carved hardstones. They were finished by the addition of a neck and rim glued into place. Their container form was more symbolic than real, their internal space was minimal, restricted to a hole drilled down the centre, and used during the carving and polishing stages as an aid to centring. (See p.56)*
British Museum, London.

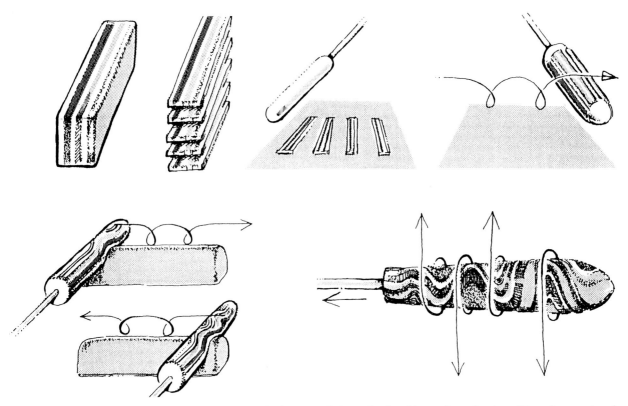

The making of a banded alabastron involves a variety of techniques relating to bead making and core-forming. Slices of contrasting glass, some encasing gold leaf, are picked up on to the surface of a core of hot glass held on a solid metal rod. These are then distorted by rolling in alternative directions along a stone shape. The resulting piece of glass is removed from the rod and ground and polished to reveal its exquisite, distorted patterns. Items like this relied on the use of small intense heat sources, probably bellows-operated, and containers to localise the heat, akin to contemporary gloryholes.

imitation of natural hard stones, but given high status in its own right. This is true of all rod-based processes and of course glass in general. The use of glass sections in high prestige artefacts like Tutankhamen's funeral mask is ample proof of this. Without this importance it is unlikely that the time, effort and sheer inventiveness would have been invested in the development of glass processes.

2 ROD-AMALGAMS

A range of procedures based on two aspects of hot glass behaviour, fusing and stretching (see opposite, left column). If rods are bundled together, using contrasting colours to create a cross-section pattern, they can be heat-fused together without losing the integrity of the original pattern. This pattern can be miniaturised at will by stretching the basic pattern to reduce its diameter. Such actions can be used in rod form in the creation of further amalgams and

stretchings. In this way enormously complex masterpieces were created. Once the various stages were invented and established the element that determined the nature of the end result was time, and for a civilisation that did not regard time as an expensive commodity the production of high-status glass objects was paramount. However, a basic description of the procedures does not do justice to the level of inventive artistry that went into their development and use. Nor does it fully describe the full range of techniques involved. The basic rod fusion and stretching technique was used to create lengths of glass which carried a complex pattern throughout their sections. Such lengths could be used to take slices from for further use. For example, symmetrical patterns could be made by placing alternative slices together with one of them reversed. Complex geometric patterns could be built from repeated segments. There were, however, other ways of creating such cross-sectioned lengths that, although not based on rod manipulation alone, deserve to be described in

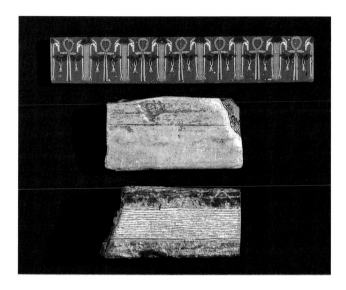

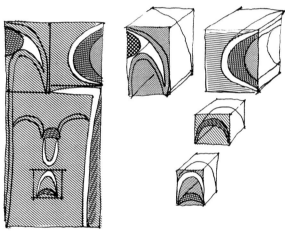

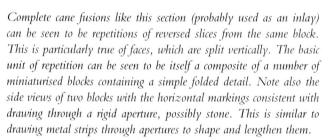

Complete cane fusions like this section (probably used as an inlay) can be seen to be repetitions of reversed slices from the same block. This is particularly true of faces, which are split vertically. The basic unit of repetition can be seen to be itself a composite of a number of miniaturised blocks containing a simple folded detail. Note also the side views of two blocks with the horizontal markings consistent with drawing through a rigid aperture, possibly stone. This is similar to drawing metal strips through apertures to shape and lengthen them.

this section. Configurations like an eye or a spiral were made by manipulating contrasting layers of glass, folding the layers over while soft to create a section in exactly the same way as a pastry cook creates a swiss roll. Such amalgams could include rods for specific details, e.g. the centre of an eye. Once created they too could be miniaturised by heating and stretching. Many such pieces have been found by Egyptologists, some with sections cut from them. These sections, the majority of which were extremely small, measuring

Alexandrian decorative plaque from the 1st century AD.

only a few centimetres, could be used on their own, or in combination with rod patterns and/or crushed glass infills to create small jewel like flat plaques (see above right and top picture overleaf). Such items were highly valued and used for the decoration of ritual rooms and objects in the service of an elite group. As P. T. Nicholson says, 'Glass probably remained a Royal Monopoly for much of the New Kingdom.' (A situation that has occurred a number of times during the history of glass, St Gobain and La Granja being examples). This fact alone justified the intense labour and application involved in their production, and to call such objects merely decorative is to undersell their role within the establishment of a religious and royal mystique. Even after the Roman conquest when rod-fused techniques were adopted to

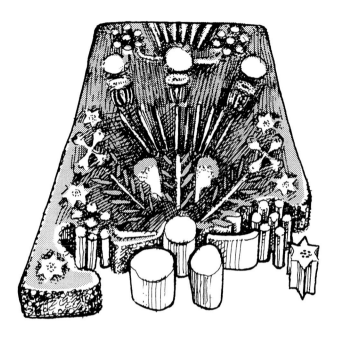

(ABOVE) *The manufacture of the decorative plaques, formed from a combination of sections cut from manipulated and pulled lengths embedded in a matrix of fused, crushed glass. These items were made to decorate flat surfaces and therefore only had to be seen from one side. The drawing shows the plaque with some of the crushed glass filling removed. This is how the pattern would have been created before fusing all of the glass components to join them into a single block, prior to grinding and polishing the top surface to reveal the pattern.*

serve a wider audience, through their use in purely luxury, secular objects, the air of exclusivity was maintained. Although container shaped, they were non-practical objects collected for their qualities and rarity value. It is hardly surprising that the rich, jewel like patterns and colours would appeal to the Roman upper-classes. This new market resulted in some important new variations of the basic New Kingdom processes which stemmed from the need to produce free standing domestic scale items, mainly bowls. These products are often described by the Renaissance term *millefiore*. I prefer to stick to the more inclusive and more accurate term rod-fused. There were, as usual, a number of distinct versions of this, but they all involved two similar stages, both using heat to trigger them (see below). The first, in which rods, or rod sections were fused into a basic shape, often a flat disc, and second, the use of a lower temperature to shape this fusion into a three dimensional form. Once achieved there invariably followed a grinding and polishing stage to remove any irregularities of surface caused during the moulding stage. The creation of hollow vessels, albeit small in scale, allowed for the development of a new variant of rod-fusion, where rods that had been twisted together were manipulated and fused to create bowls formed by a rod or series of rods spiralling horizontally to create the walls. These so called *reticelli* bowls (see opposite, right) are

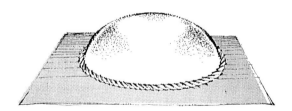

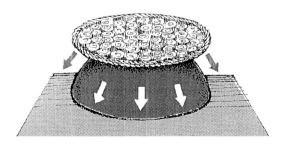

(BELOW LEFT) *The creation of a rod-fused bowl could have been achieved using a number of related techniques. They all involved the making of a fused disc from the various rod sections which was then distorted by bending over, into, or through a former. Here a twisted rod rim is first made to determine the eventual diameter of the bowl. This is used to hold the rod sections as they fuse, and the resulting disc is shaped over a stone or ceramic mould. The way in which the rod pattern distorts as it becomes three dimensional displays the precise way in which it has been shaped. Sections slumped into a mould will be compressed; those laid over a mould will be stretched.*

(ABOVE) *An Alexandrian* reticelli *bowl from the 1st century* AD. *The adaptation of Egyptian rod-formed techniques to serve a new Roman market.*

British Museum, London.

(ABOVE) *A sandwich glass bowl. This complex and rare object comprises two separate layers of clear glass with a gold leaf pattern sandwiched between them. The leaf must have been applied cold to the surface of the lower glass layer, as the pattern has been carefully scratched out, a process needing considerable time. The secondary layer of glass has been fused onto the first, a process requiring a high level of heat. The entire inside and outside surfaces of the bowl have been painstakingly ground and polished. Gold leaf is easily destroyed by heat, and the fusion of the two layers must have occurred quickly and expertly. A similar technique was employed in the manufacture of the discs of glass with gold leaf trapped between. I would presume the technique to be as follows: a sheet of cold glass is covered with gold leaf and the pattern scratched out, the disc is warmed to prevent thermal shock and a layer of hot glass applied, this sandwich disc is slumped over a former and, lastly, ground and polished. The resulting bowl was always fragile and non-functional. It demonstrates the lengths that Roman craftsmen were prepared to go to achieve a particular effect.*

Pilkington Glass Museum.

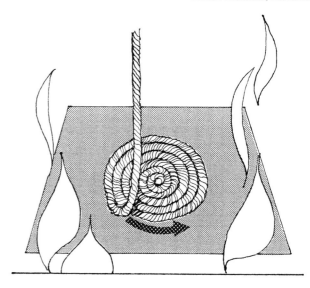

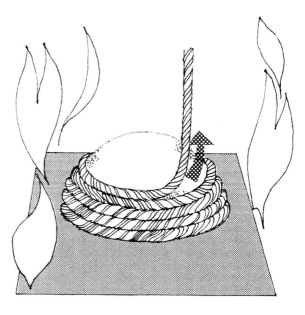

(LEFT) *The production of* reticelli *bowls required the building of an open, three dimensional form from twisted glass rods. There are a number of ways in which this can be achieved, although it is difficult to glean too much from surviving examples, as it was common practice to grind and polish the entire interior and exterior surfaces, thereby removing important traces of manufacture. A length of twisted rod could be heated to soften it; it could either be coiled onto a flat surface to make a disc which would be subsequently bent over a former, or coiled directly onto a former. Both of these procedures would have required a small, open-topped kiln to achieve the necessary heat.*

A slumped bowl from the 1st century AD. *Made from a fusion of loosely folded sections of differently coloured glass. These may represent the end areas of pulled rods which have not been miniaturised during the process of manufacture.*

The British Museum, London.

astonishing objects which still deny us total understanding of their manufacturing methods (see previous page, left). They do however find contemporary counterparts in the work of glass artists of the stature of Toots Zynsky and Klaus Moje who, despite being at a distance of two thousand years from them, use exactly the same basic methods to produce similar objects.

CASTING

One fact makes any speculation about the precise casting procedures used in the Ancient World difficult. All objects made by casting have been ground and polished over their entire surface, thereby removing all traces that could act as clues to the exact method used. As usual it is helpful to look at the cultural and material contexts for clues about the background to the process. Not only was glass a material allied to luxury and exclusivity – it was never used to form functional, practical objects. Even the ostensibly functional core-formed vessels were produced for an elite and served primarily as symbolic status symbols. The range of forms that

casting was used to produce was small and often solid, deriving from the use of stone and its lapidary shaping techniques. As a result, casting seems to have been used for the production of relatively simple shapes of no great size or complexity during the New Kingdom, which represents the apogee of Egyptian glassmaking. The Egyptians had by then developed a long tradition of stone carving and polishing, and glass casting fitted into this. Casts were simple, crude shapes that represented an approximation of the final object, and which relied almost entirely on carving and polishing for their final shape and surface. Well known items like the Sargon vase or Tutankhamen's headrest are of this kind and the extent of the carving and polishing has led some historians to speculate (particularly in the case of the Sargon vase) that such objects were in fact carved from a rough lump of glass rather than cast, although this is unlikely as even an approximate cast would have made its production much easier. The headrest clearly shows its cast origins by being constructed from two identical cast pieces, joined in the middle with a gold mount.[13]

Casting involves melting glass ingots, pieces, rods or grains into a mould which provides the shape of the desired glass piece. In order to make the glass fill the mould the temperature must be raised and kept to a high level. At such a temperature the glass loses all of its original surface and picks up the texture of the mould material. In the Ancient World mould materials would have been fairly unsophisticated, probably based on ceramic mixes, and would have contaminated the glass surface. This would have made it essential for the object to be ground and polished over its entire surface. It is highly likely that precious metal casting provided the technology and expertise for glass casting, and there is some evidence to support the idea. Certainly casting precious metals involved the lost-wax process where an original, modelled in soft wax would be embedded in a ceramic mix and melted out through an aperture. Molten metal (or glass) would be introduced into the mould through this aperture to fill the void previously occupied by the 'lost' wax. Gold casting, which like most processes pre-dated its use for glassforming, also possessed the kiln and heating technology required. Metal, however, flows more readily than glass and it is the

A cast bowl produced by the Achaemenid Persians in the 5th century BC. Such a glass object exactly follows the forms of those produced in silver and bronze. It is reasonable to presume that the blank form was produced by lost-wax casting and the final surface and details realised by cutting and polishing. Lost-wax casting remains one of the most difficult of glassforming processes, and vessels such as this represent the first high point of casting. They must have been cast in closed moulds, in order to shape the whole three-dimensional form, with the minimum access to introduce the glass. Their relatively large size (this one is 17.2 cm in diameter) make their production even more remarkable.
The Toledo Museum of Art, USA.

work of seconds to fill even a complex mould from a crucible of molten metal. The casting of glass is a much slower process, involving as it does the gradual feeding of glass into the mould while subjecting it to continuous heating over a long period. The complexity of the shape to be cast and the number and size of the apertures (sprues) determines the ease of casting and the length of the casting process. This is why so many Egyptian objects were cast as simple flat-backed forms. This avoided the need for complex casting openings and meant that the mould was, effectively, open. In such castings glass ingots could be placed directly into the mould rather than through narrow apertures.

Although casting was used for the partial manufacture of special objects it was the Achaemenid dynasty of the Persian civilisation (see above) that established it as a major forming method in its own right during the 7th century BC. Their incredible and, in terms of survival, rare cast bowls follow precisely, well-established gold and silver

versions, further lending credibility to the idea that they were made by goldsmiths. Their forms (and scale) are much more complex than anything cast by the Egyptians, and must have required a sophisticated understanding of the nature and behaviour of viscous glass. Despite the fact that the mould and glass would have had to be held at a damaging high temperature for many hours the quality of the cast and glass are extremely high. The surviving examples have all been ground and polished to bring up the surface and to sharpen the details of the modelling. This too is consistent with the treatment of cast gold and silver forms which were also ground and polished to remove mould dullness. One of the wonderful aspects of glass history is that it is not necessarily a story of continuous improvement, and despite their extreme age the products of Mesopotamia, Egypt and Persia in the millennia before the birth of Christ are undoubted masterpieces and remain unsurpassed despite technical advances.

Alexandrian fuse-cast footed container made around the time of the birth of Christ. The sections of patterned rod are fused and manipulated on a central rod to create a piece of glass that is ground and polished to reveal its pattern. The internal space is minimal and based on the rod used in its manufacture.
Bristol Museums and Art Gallery.

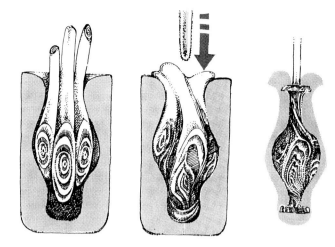

The creation of the blank for the rare item shown on the previous page. Pieces of folded rod section (possibly the larger sections left at the ends of pulled rods) are fused into an approximate shape within a two-piece stone or ceramic mould. When fused, this is picked up on a metal rod, and the mould broken away. On cooling, the glass is lathe turned (using the rod) and polished. The rod is removed creating the nominal internal spaces that are characteristic of this small group of objects.

Our interpretation and accounts of ancient glass-processes are based on the accidental survival of objects and texts. Our ideas are, therefore, incomplete and must be capable of constant revision as new evidence comes to light. There already exist anomalous facts that do necessarily fit into our versions of ancient history. For instance archaeologists have discovered a massive piece of glass that could not have been made by accident and must at least have been an experiment if not a normal procedure. It could have been a method for mass producing raw glass for breaking into pieces for trade, but its sheer scale suggests that the knowledge of and attitude to glass of the Egyptians may well need reviewing at a future date.[14]

As usual glass does not fit neatly into the categories we invent for it and there exist a further group of objects and processes that belong somewhere between fused amalgams and genuine casting. This variant involves the 'fuse casting' (see opposite and above) of objects by filling a mould with separate sections of glass (usually canes) and heating them until they join together to create a complete form. In this version of casting, however, the individual pieces of glass remain in evidence as a complex pattern that runs throughout the body of

the cast. Their manufacture must have involved the filling of the mould with carefully cut and positioned glass pieces prior to heating. The particular qualities of such objects stem from the early relationship of glass to semi-precious hardstones and the way in which these were lovingly carved to reveal their much-prized colour and internal structures. Despite their origins in mimicry these objects and their processes were also essentially 'glassy' in method and outcome.

As usual, the direction one approaches glass from largely determines the view taken of it, and which of its myriad qualities are valued and exploited. In the Ancient World (occupying a much longer time frame than the modern world to date) the ways in which glass developed were given their initial momentum from the pre-existence of ceramic, metal and stone. As I have already stated, it would be impossible to imagine the development of core-forming without the framework of processes that provided its direct antecedents. Despite the fact that glass invariably develops within well-established societies and begins by borrowing both technology and forms from other materials its essential character soon emerges. A shift of circumstances occurred with the destruction of the Ancient World, and its replacement by a unified outgoing one based upon Roman domination of the Mediterranean. Roman civilisation provided a ready market for high quality secular glass items. This in turn encouraged the development of new processes and a more centralised approach to glassmaking.

For the first time the production of large numbers of similar items became an economic aim, and genuinely industrial systems were created. This began with the processes of bending, also called sagging or slumping, (see overleaf) where a disc of glass was formed, through heat and gravity, over a mould made from fired clay or cut stone. This technique was probably derived from the similar forming of a metal blank over a mandrel by hammering. The bowls, made in glass by deforming the heat softened disc over a mould, were still individually made and would still have been exclusive items, produced for a social elite.

The glass bowls were finished by grinding and polishing inside, to remove mould marking, and were often completed by the addition of a single

A rib-moulded bowl made by slumping a disc, and shaped by pressing hot glass poured from a crucible. The ribs were created during pressing by slots in the tool; they help the disc to form accurately over the mould. The rim area and the internal surfaces have been subsequently ground and polished to remove marks of moulding and irregularities caused by slumping. These objects have a particular formal and textural character which result from this method, and are anything but inferior versions of later, blown forms.
Bristol Museums and Art Gallery.

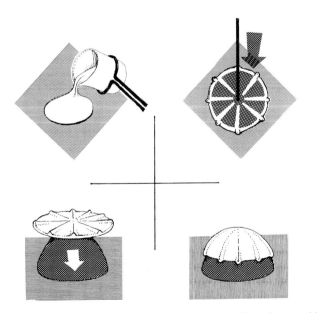

Stages in the production of a ribbed bowl. A disc of hot glass would be created by pouring hot glass on to a flat stone surface. This would be pressed with a flat, disc-shaped stone, ceramic or metal former which had a number of radial grooves or slits cut into it. This created a disc of glass with raised radiating ribs which was bent over a mould. The resulting bowl was ground internally, and the rim area cut to create an even profile.

horizontal ground band. In this and their general profiles, they copied metal originals – another clue as to their origins. However, the material of glass transformed the metal original into the unique single colour, refined vessels that characterise this process.

The great shift in manufacturing methods that occurred in response to the influence of the Roman Empire also helped to redefine glass. Instead of being prized for its rarity, collected as precious and mysterious, it became associated with useful everyday activities and commonplace containers. This revolution in use and perception, giving rise to the claim that during the Roman Empire glass could be bought for 'the price of a copper coin'[15] was brought about by the invention of arguably the most essentially 'glassy' process of all – inflation (see p.65). Glassblowing is so firmly associated with the material that it and its products are practically synonymous with it, certainly in terms of our own era. The qualities most frequently associated with

Glassblowing, Chance Bros, 1930. The basis of this process is the creation of a bubble of viscous glass. This image shows the unfettered expansion of the bubble as part of crown glass production.
Pilkington Bros Ltd Archive.

glass, transparency and fragility, are those most characteristic of blown objects. Despite this, it is worth stressing again that the process was not invented until glass had been in independent existence for over three millennia – a period in which qualities other than transparency were sought after and valued. It is worth speculating about how and why it first came into being. Although it can rightly lay claim to prime status, it is alone of all the major glassforming processes in that there are no accounts of or clues to its origins or antecedents. Any study of the history of invention suggests that few, if any, discoveries occur in isolation or emerge without a period of experimental development. New processes are invariably simply new ways of looking at or assembling established customs and practices. Most registered patents describe their originality as mere improvements to existing procedures in recognition of this fact. Yet despite this, glassblowing is so radical, and its first appearance so complete that it literally divides the

history of the material in two, for nothing in glass remained the same after its use became common and widespread. Once established it dominated glassforming and glassforms, holding a pre-eminent position, to the virtual exclusion of all others, from some time around the birth of Christ until the late 17th century. This was not until the first attempts occurred in 1688 to produce flat mirror glass away from the dominance of the glass house, in which the techniques of blowing reigned supreme. The first effect of its move to dominance in the 1st century AD was the demise of the processes that had served the Ancient World, particularly core-forming and mosaic-fusion. Glassblowing, its methods and products were derived from the circumstances and product requirements of the New World order. As with all important technical developments (and in terms of the history of glass, the most important), it was the result of a number of social, economic and material circumstances. The natural product of the inflation of a bubble of glass is a container, a product that was eagerly sought by the centralised Roman Empire. Its development seems logical from our point of view, as direct heirs to the Roman system, but we should be cautious of viewing it as the invention that superseded all previous processes. I actually prefer the term development to invention as I believe that glassblowing emerged fully formed when it did because circumstances made it necessary. Core-forming and rod-fusion were well suited to the needs of the societies they served; our contemporary notions of speed, repeatability and efficiency are the incorrect criteria to judge all processes equally. What is remarkable about glassblowing is the speed at which its necessary tools and skills developed. Although some were adapted from other uses (glassmakers' shears, for example, are identical to sheep shears) most were like the physical skills themselves, too specialised to have enjoyed a previous existence. The prime use to which glassblowing was put was the production of containers, the shapes of which already belonged to other materials, particularly ceramic. Yet despite the fact that glassblowing began by imitating these in glass it was not long before they were either transformed through the vocabulary of glass, or new generic glass shapes emerged. It is impossible to overemphasise the creative way in which the early glass blowers responded so quickly and inventively to this new process.

THE BASIC PRINCIPLES

Glass is a unique material, a supercooled liquid, that is to say one that has cooled too quickly and to too low a temperature to freeze in a conventional sense. Its molecules simply stop moving without forming themselves into the normal crystalline lattice matrix of a solid; this is one reason why glass can be transparent. Its cooling process, from maximum liquidity to solidity, is gradual and characterised by its behaviour as an elastic mobile mass that loses its ability to move as it loses temperature. This mobile mass is given form by the way in which cooling glass creates a skin at its junction with a cooler medium. In practice this is usually the air in which the

glassblower moves the glass mass on the end of the blowpipe, but the working of hot glass by contact with moulds, tools or machinery also help to leach heat from it and to cause the formation of a skin. In fact, without this combination of mobility and surface skin no glass processes, least of all blowing could have developed in the forms they did. During the three millennia of its use prior to glassblowing all of the processes in use relied on this basic property, but none exploited it in the way glassblowing did. The process relies on the introduction of a small amount of air into an amount of liquid, but coherent, blob of glass. This has the effect of creating an elastic skin on the inside of the bubble to match the exterior caused by removal from the furnace (see opposite). This creates a natural, basic container form that can be increased in size by expanding the amount of air trapped within the bubble (see opposite). It is hard to find any antecedents for this process; it requires a metal tube to both gather the glass on and through which to introduce and increase the air. Metal tubes clearly pre-dated glassblowing. They were made with difficulty, by wrapping a heated strip round a mandrel, and were probably used in processes like metal founding and distilling. There is some speculation that the first blown glass was made by inflating the closed ends of glass tubes. This is certainly feasible technically and is used today by lampworkers. If true, it would certainly have provided a convenient catalyst for the invention of blowing, but it has for me a major drawback. The production of glass tubing on the scale required was, until our own era, produced exclusively by glassblowing and I can find no evidence for its production prior to it.[16] In any case, for glassblowing to develop into the multi-layered process it was to become the use of metal tube was essential. The use of a tube (blowing iron) enables the elaboration of the basic process into further sophisticated forming methods. For a start, it allows the addition of further layers (gathers) of hot glass to the original bubble. However, before discussing the development of the of the full blowing process it would seem important to mention the necessary, allied changes to the technology of the material that accompanied its rise to dominance.

Automated blowing at Schott in Germany. The lungs and manual control systems inherent in a human craftsman have been replaced by compressed air and hydraulic and electric motors. Such mechanised systems, unlike manual skill, lack the ability to adjust to variations and rely on rigorous repetition of all aspects of the operation.

Schott Glass, Germany.

MATERIAL PROVISION

Glassmaking in the Ancient World was carried out within a decentralised system. Glass shaping was often separate from glassmaking and the raw forms of glass (rod, lump and ingot) were made in a glass foundry and could be transported over large distances to the workshop that gave it its final form. Glassblowing on the other hand required that hot liquid glass be made and worked in the same building. This led to the establishment of factory conditions as early as AD100 and set the fixed, static nature of glassblowing workshops for the next two thousand years. Many establishments still set great store by their continuity on one site over many centuries.[17]

The centralised, static nature of the glass factory was caused partly by the process and also by the new scale and numbers of glass objects required. The constant need for containers caused improvements to the process of founding liquid glass through the provision of efficient furnaces and the ceramic pots used to melt the raw materials. The glass of the pre-Christian era required only small, temporary furnaces, but glassblowing required a constant supply of liquid glass to feed the glass workers processes. The workforce too was now part of the factory and it also developed into dynasties of glass workers centred on particular sites.

Once temperature is reached, sufficient to turn the ingredients into liquid glass, it is important for its structure and materials that it is kept running at a consistently high temperature, even broken pots had to be replaced while the furnace was running (see below). This fact dictated many of the characteristics of blown glass production, not only its association over many centuries with particular sites, but also its adherence to rigid production cycles like those used by the medieval forest glassmakers.

The large ceramic container (pot) of liquid glass had to allow access for the blowing iron to dip in and rotate to pick up (gather) glass on its end despite the heat loss that this entails. The temperature had to be maintained at the maximum level possible, for although glass can only be produced by heating the raw ingredients to 1100°C (2012°F), the maximum that could be achieved and sustained at the time was little over 1000°C (1832°F). To counter this problem the first glassblowers devised a clever two-stage process that remained in use until the 17th century.[18] In this, the basic ingredients were partially melted to remove impurities and start the chemical and physical transformation of the raw materials into their synthesis as glass. This stage was known as fritting and was an essential part of the glassmaking process until improvements in furnace design, ceramic technology and fuel made it possible to reach and maintain high enough temperatures to found glass in one operation. Once fritted the partially fused ingredients were cooled and ground to a sand-like consistency before re-heating to found true glass.

The continuous nature of glass production systems centred on the provision of hot glass for glassblowing, and is dramatically illustrated by the pot-changing system within a traditional glasshouse (in this case Chance Bros, around 1930). A broken pot had to be removed and a new one installed without turning the furnace off, and the massive steel frame was designed to facilitate both removal and replacement. It was wielded by a team of glass workers wearing water-soaked clothes who also took down and replaced the brick wall of the furnace in a relay.
Pilkington Bros Ltd Archive.

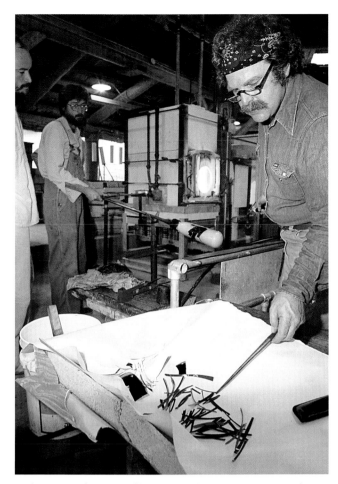

Joel Myers making one of his renowned Fragments *series. The process he evolved to create the unique painterly effects involves the production of special glass fragments which he carefully positions on the blown bubble, fusing them into the surface with a blowtorch.*
Courtesy Joel Phillip Myers.

This stage enabled the impurities produced to burn off without becoming trapped into the glass, and fritting pans were shallow to present a large surface area to the heat. In addition to the two separate chambers for fritting and final founding, the early furnaces had to provide two further heat facilities, both essential in the glassmaking process, these were re-heating and annealing. Once glass is removed from the heated pot on the end of the blowing iron it begins to lose heat and elasticity, yet it is only while in an elastic state that it can be shaped by inflation and have extra glass added to it. The period from liquidity to rigidity is known as the working time and can be extended by re-heating. This can be achieved by placing it back in the furnace mouth or by adding an extra layer of hot glass. Later in its history a separate chamber was built especially for this stage, it was called a glory-hole and since the development of gas as a fuel has become a freestanding structure, separate from the main furnace. The use of hand-held gas torches in the glasshouse for selectively heating areas of the glass is a further, contemporary sophistication (see above and overleaf).

A further chamber was required, heated by the excess heat of the furnace, in which the glass products were brought to room temperature. This process, called annealing, is essential to even-out the stresses within the glass and is now achieved with pin-point scientific accuracy in a separate structure (lehr) in which the glass products move through the required heat levels on a conveyor belt. In Roman times (and up to the 19th century) this was achieved by cruder means. The glass objects were moved gradually to the front of the chamber, and devices like cobblestones were placed within its area to retain heat and distribute it more evenly. Like most glass procedures prior to our own era, it was made effective by observation and constant repetition.

The importance of the furnace, and the extreme difficulties associated with its maintenance, dictated the static nature of glassblowing, and created

69

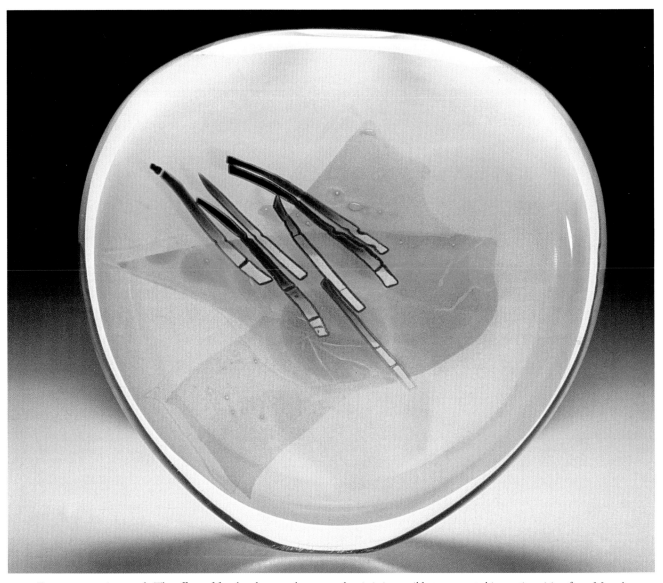

Fragments series vessel. The effects of fused, colour overlay mean that it is impossible to separate his creative vision from Myers'
personal working method.
Courtesy Joel Phillip Myers.

circumstances whereby all objects that needed to be produced from hot glass had to be made within the same building. This effectively caused a revolution in glass making, one that was to dominate it for the best part of two thousand years. In effect, the setting up of glass factories in the 1st century AD predated the establishment of factories for the working of other materials in the Industrial Revolution of the 18th and 19th centuries. The senate in Rome issued an edict in AD 100 forcing glass factories to move at least a mile from the city centre because of the smoke from their furnaces. All glass products had to be designed from a base line of the facilities, skills, and tools used within these factories. Not only was a

blown bubble an archetypal container, but glass was also the ideal container material. It did not contaminate contents, particularly liquids; it could be made quickly, in a single operation, unlike ceramic which required glazing to achieve true impermeability. The full range of glassblowing techniques developed within a few decades of its introduction, allowed it to be used in an immense variety of ways, resulting in the standardised production of a vast range of glass containers. This, and the nature of glassblowing itself helped to establish glass as a predominantly transparent material for the first time in its long existence. Blowing glass automatically creates a hollow form with thin walls through which light passes. Control over the extent of this transparency became a central issue for the next two thousand years.

EXTENSIONS TO THE BASIC BUBBLE

Although the invention of glassforming by inflation remains, arguably, the most singular event in the history of glass, it would not, on its own, have achieved this status. To convert a simple bubble into a practical, recognisable container required the invention of a range of supporting procedures involving skill and a number of equally specialised tools. Given that almost all of these had to be devised from scratch with few references to other material systems, their development was, in many ways, as remarkable as the invention of blowing itself. Within a very few years the whole basic range of glassmaking skills and techniques were in use, and while variants of them have been, and continue to be, developed by successive generations, few add much to the basic principles devised by the early Syrian glassmakers. These comprise a small number of crucial additions to the basic bubble.

OPENING THE BUBBLE

This involves transferring the bubble from its hollow iron to a solid rod attached by a sticky blob of hot glass to its other end. This allows the opening created by its removal from the blowing iron to be re-heated and opened out. This process, which owes nothing to any other material, makes use of four particularly 'glassy' characteristics, and establishes principles that form the basis of all subsequent additional procedures (see right).

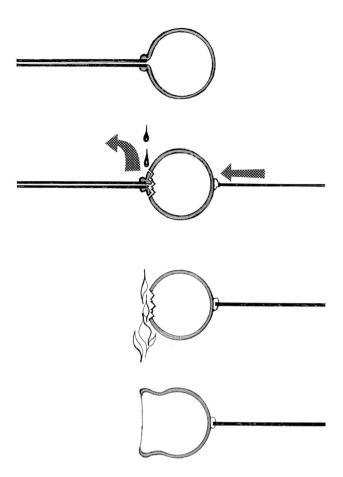

Puntying. The method by which the original blown glass bubble is transferred from the hollow iron to a solid punty iron, attached a small gather of hot glass. This procedure is second only to the bubble itself in importance for, without it, it would not be possible to make most free-blown vessel forms. It enables the production of items such as jugs and bowls which require the opening up and shaping of the area originally attached to the iron.

(RIGHT) *The base of an 18th-century bottle showing the domed base and the remains of the punty. The raised 'kick' in the base of such containers served two functions: to stabilise the weight distribution of the liquid, and to enable the punty mark to lift clear of the surface on which the bottle was placed. The residue of the punty, shown as bright fragments of broken glass, indicates that the punty was a disc of glass that only adhered to the bottle where its circumference met the dome at its base.*

Broadfield House Glass Museum. Photo, David Jones.

1 *Puntying.* The attachment of the bubble to the solid punty rod to allow its removal from the iron. This makes use of the fact that the original bubble has dropped enough in temperature to be solid, but is still hot enough to stick to a small, liquid blob of hot glass at the end of the punty iron.

2 *Cracking off.* The use of water to create a crack at the point where the bubble is connected to the blowing iron.

3 *Re-heating.* The fact that glass can be re-heated many times to restore its original plasticity and allow reshaping and/or the addition of new glass.

4 *Shearing.* (see right) This makes use of the highly individual nature of soft glass whereby it can be cut with shears. This, which is directly attributable to the surface skin of glass is a major component of numerous glassmaking systems.

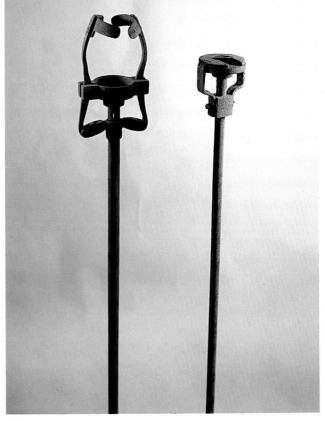

These four basic principles relate to the shaping of the original bubble, but this is extended by additions of hot glass in ways that allow a particular vocabulary of forms. On the face of it, these seem to be restricted to variations of a simple blob of hot glass, until the ways in which this has been exploited are considered. A hot blob can be obviously varied in size and, once attached to the original bubble, can be reformed in either a static or mobile way. Static, it can be re-shaped with pincers, elongated using gravity, pressed with a hand-held prunting device or crimped. Mobile it can, through stretching, be wound into a trailed, elongated thread. (see p.47). These basic ways of attaching and re-shaping simple

The addition of a single blob of hot glass to the wall of a vessel during manufacture has been constantly exploited over two millennia, to yield some of the most characteristic and individual glass decorations. This example of a single prunt impressed with a lion's head was made by Thomas Webb in the 1870s.

Broadfield House Museum. Photo, David Jones.

Ice-glass. A technique which uses two contradictory aspects of glass to create a decorative effect. A bubble of glass is plunged into water and shatters, but the shards hold together because it is done quickly. This is then re-heated to fuse the fragments without losing the shattered effect.

Broadfield House Museum. Photo, David Jones.

blobs of hot glass accounted for both functional and decorative detailing, rims, handles, feet, trails and prunts (see above, left) used either separately or in combination to achieve complex effects. The act of adding a small blob of extra glass could be repeated many times as long as the glass attached to the iron was kept warm.

Although the forms of early containers and the way in which details like handles, feet and spouts were added and shaped were originally based on the shapes of containers made from ceramic, metal and wood, it is a tribute to the inventiveness of the early glassmakers that they rapidly re-expressed these forms and details through the novel language of glass. This was particularly true of details like handles, where

straightforward copies of ceramic or metal versions would have served the practical purpose. Instead, there is a creative, playful aesthetic enjoyment at work from the earliest glass production. The glassmakers quickly learned to express the liquid nature of glass and to celebrate the way in which this could be frozen permanently into the finished object (see above and overleaf). The evidence of an experimental approach to this new material, despite the extreme limitations imposed by the practical nature of the containers seem to confirm Huizinga's definition of man as *Homo Ludens*:[19] man the player rather than solely man the maker or thinker.

In order to carry out these new techniques a system of unconscious bodily movements had to be

A 19th-century novelty decanter called a Kuttrolf. *The complex form of the container is created by exploiting the nature of glassblowing. Just as forms are created by inflating softened glass, so they can also be subjected to distortion through deflation. Here the walls of a square bottle are pulled back by the glassmaker sucking the air out of the glass while the walls are still mobile. The resulting configuration makes it difficult to pour liquid evenly from the vessel. The technique and shape are as old as glassblowing and the name* Kuttrolf *is reckoned to be based on the noise made when the vessel is used.*
Broadfield House Museum. Photo, David Jones.

(ABOVE) *The glassmaker's chair. Developed during the Renaissance, possibly in Italy, it is both simple and highly sophisticated. It evolved as a substitute for the use of the human body as a platform for glassmaking. The two parallel bars that act as a guide and support for the rolling blowing iron were originally provided by the thighs of the glassmaker. These were supplemented by wooden runners strapped to the thighs prior to the final development of the chair.*

Royal Brierley Crystal. Photo, David Jones.

(RIGHT) *Here a jug is completed by the casting on of a handle pulled from a single blob of hot glass.*

Photo, Janet Elliott.

developed and mastered (see above, right). Prior to the development of glassblowing such movements that were used to control soft liquid glass were confined to the hands and arms, but glassblowing demanded a range of full body movements that could be used to keep the mobile glass stable as a form on the iron. Furthermore, these movements had to be controlled automatically while the actual shaping took place. To keep the mobile soft glass stable a series of constant adjustments and corrections had to take place to prevent unwanted distortion and movement. This is mainly achieved by

rotating the iron horizontally, originally sitting on a stool and using the thighs as runners. This developed by the Middle Ages into the use of wooden runners strapped to the thighs, and by the Renaissance into a glassmaker's chair that included the runners (see above, left). The development of this chair is analogous to the development of the potter's wheel, and there are indeed many similarities between blowing glass and throwing clay, however the differences are also of interest. Whereas the potter operates through a direct access to the material via the hands, the glassmaker can only exercise control

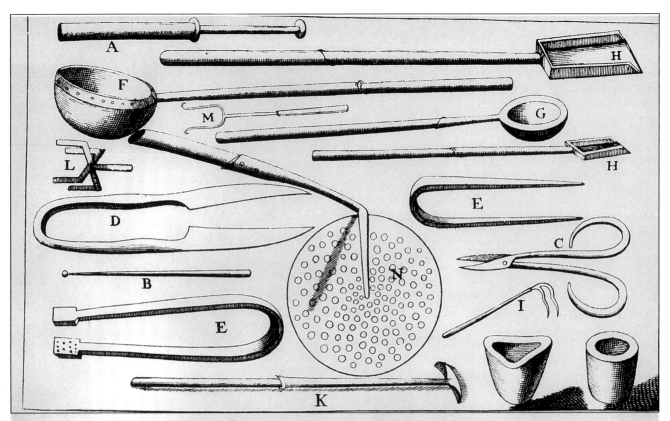

Fig. 17. Glass-making tools.

A, Blowing-iron. B, Pontee or puntee. C, Scissors. D, Shears or shaping-tool. E—N, pincers, ladles, shovels, drainers and other implements used in glass-making in the seventeenth century. Blancourt's *Art of Glass*.

Glassmaking tools. These have remained virtually unchanged since their origins some 2000 years ago, and many, like the pucellas, *are still known worldwide by their original Latin names.*
Pilkington Bros Ltd Archive.

through the use of tools (see above) that are, in effect extensions of lungs and hands. Physical movements can be used to deliberately distort the glass as well as keeping it stable, the elongation of the bubble by swinging it on the end of the iron is an example. It is this ballet of co-ordinated physical skills that makes glassblowing such an interesting activity to watch and why its exponents often relish an audience. The activity carries with it the drama of something being produced in real time with a constant risk of failure. It also links those who possess these skills in a special way. A friend of mine, a skilled gaffer, went to visit a famous glass factory in America. In the glasshouse he asked if he could try the glass. After making a gather and starting to blow, the local craftsman who had been watching carefully, announced loudly 'It's OK, he's one of us'.

The free blowing of hot glass involves nothing

more than the operation of the skilled use of a range of simple tools that are extensions of the glassmaker. It is, in glass terms, the most direct relationship between maker and material; a dialogue that results in the creation of an object in one session. Because free blown glass is shaped primarily by its movement through the air and the expansion of the air inside it, its surfaces remain close to its liquid origins. The skin that occurs as the glass cools is allowed to form freely, and as a result *free* blown forms are the purest in traditional 'glassy', terms, being shiny, flawless and above all, transparent. It is not surprising that the aesthetic theorists of the modern movement like Morris and Ruskin felt that free blown glass that kept close to the original bubble form represented the *apogee* of glassmaking. They felt that the forms that resulted were truer to the nature of glass than methods that were less direct, saving their especial scorn for processes, such as wheel cutting, that were used to decorate and destroy the purity of free blown forms. The fact that Ruskin cited the unpleasant high-pitched noises made while glass was cut as a reason to condemn its results indicates another set of values at work.

There is no doubt that the beauty and drama of the physical choreography involved in the blowing of glass possesses a strong performance value that spills over to the objects made from it. It helped to make a visit to a glasshouse part of the original grand tour and is a feature of most contemporary studios and factories, where it is often a useful marketing tool. Samuel Pepys found a visit to a London glass house to watch some of his wine bottles blown, an event worth noting in his Diary.[20] In our own post-industrial society those makers who work glass by hand skills utilise the performance quality of these to add status to their products. The visual drama of making has, in such cases, become inseparable from its end result. No matter how often it is seen it always impresses and excites by its combination of skill and danger. It epitomises David Pye's definition of hand driven craft as being the 'workmanship of risk'.[21] It is not until our own era that glassmaking skills and personal control over the outcome of these skills has been allowed to reside in the same person. Prior to our own era, glassblowers were largely anonymous artisans whose function was to produce objects whose forms were dictated to them, the exceptions, such as Ennion and Barovier, simply serve to emphasise the fact. There is always an element of pride in craftsmanship in even the most prescribed and anonymous glass object. It is one reason for the inventiveness shown in the forms of simple details like handles, and also shows itself in the production, through the ages of objects called 'friggers'. These were objects made by glassmakers for their own use and amusement. Despite having no practical function, they often aped functional objects, pipes, walking sticks, hats etc. Their production, which is remarkably widespread, perhaps went some way towards countering the pressures of serial production and to celebrate the individual skill behind it. Despite its special qualities as a process it was nevertheless originally developed primarily as a mass production method, and ways were sought and developed by the early glassmakers to speed up its processes and standardise its products. This is why, in addition to free blowing, mould blowing developed alongside it, from, as far as we can see, earliest times.

MOULD BLOWING

To determine the final shape of a bubble of glass, not by manual skill, but by inflating it into a mould of some kind is a less spectacular but no less radical way of forming than free blowing (see overleaf). Like most hot glass processes it has few antecedents in the forming repertoires of other materials, the nearest being the liquid casting of metals or ceramic slip into moulds. Its appearance so soon after the development of glassblowing is remarkable in itself, but it is more than matched by the way in which its full potential was realised and exploited so quickly. Although its main benefits were its ability to standardise container forms, speed up their manufacture and do so with less reliance on skill, mould blowing also made possible important additions to the formal vocabulary of glassblowing. The outside shape of the mould could be determined by the shape of the mould rather than the skill of the blower. This in turn offered a way to escape the overwhelming influence of centrifugal symmetry. The shape and texture of the glass is determined by the designer/maker of the mould rather than the movements of the blower. If free blowing is an example of David Pye's 'workmanship of risk' then mould blowing is a significant move towards his 'workmanship of certainty'. (In terms of the production of glass containers this was fully achieved by Michael Owens's bottle-making machine in the early 20th century; see p.79.) Mould blowing can be used to produce perfectly symmetrical forms that imitate those made by free blown methods, although the results are more regular and lack the sparkle of a free blown surface. It is, however when moulds are used to form shapes that cannot be produced by hand that the technique reveals its own vocabulary of possibilities.

Within its range there exists a number of separate formal categories based on variations of the basic technique: 1) Turn-round, 2) Still-blown: Single piece and 3) Still-blown: Multi-piece. Early

Giving shape to a glass bubble by inflating it into a mould. This Roman beaker was blown into a hand-modelled, fired clay mould, which, because of the relief decoration on its surface, had to be split into two halves to allow the glass to be removed. 1st century AD.
Photo, Derek Balmer.

mould systems drew from the established technologies of metal, wood, and especially ceramic, which was the most flexible.

above right). This can be enhanced by the use of mould coatings, or even the simple addition of a small piece of wet paper to create steam to act as both buffer and lubricant.

1 TURN-ROUND

As the name suggests such moulds allow the glass bubble to be rotated in the mould as it is inflated, and can only be used in the production of symmetrical forms with no texture. Turning the glass round has the effect of smoothing and polishing the surface of the glass by not allowing it to stay in direct contact with the mould surface (see

2 STILL-BLOWN: SINGLE PIECE

Shapes produced by this method are those which, by their profile and/or surface texture do not allow movement during the inflation of the bubble, but because they are straight sided allow the completed shape to be removed in one movement by pulling it upwards from the single piece mould (see above).

A group of Roman bottles from the 2nd and 3rd centuries AD. *They demonstrate the advantages of blown glass as a medium for the mass production of containers. They are all mould blown, which ensures a standardisation of shape, and details are added through manipulated trails of soft glass. The handles are formed with care to avoid destroying the verticality of their outline. This ensures that they can be stacked closely together during storage and transit. Although strictly practical they have an austere beauty which is enhanced by the blue and green glass used to make them.*
The Toledo Museum of Art, USA.

The production of square and rectangular containers were the first examples of such items, designed to allow their face to face storage and transportation (see above). Their practical origins, and relative technical simplicity do not detract from either their beauty or originality within glass history.

(RIGHT) *A split mould with the finished article made from it. The mould-shaped body of the decanter, which then had its neck formed (after puntying) and its flat sides polished. This is a fine example of the use of a mould to give form to an object that is radically different to that possible by free blowing.*
Royal Brierley Crystal Ltd. Photo, David Jones.

(ABOVE) *The famous vase designed by Alvar Aalto in 1937 for the Savoy Hotel. His use of an asymmetric mould made from steam-bent wood was inspired by his use of the same technology for his bent wood furniture. The mould now used is cast iron, but like its wooden ancestor is a simple, vertical pull-out mould. The form is not puntied. The 'blow over' is cut off and the rim polished.*
Broadfield House Glass Museum. Photo, David Jones.

3 STILL-BLOWN: MULTI-PIECE

For still-blown forms which could not be pulled out straight from a one piece mould, sectioned moulds had to be produced to allow the glass to be removed (see previous page, lower picture). Such a system had to be capable of easy break-down and re-assembly, and ceramic was an ideal material as it could be hand-modelled, pressed or slab built in sections and fired to render it semi-permanent.

The use of sectioned and multi-piece moulds allowed the development of surface modelling and texture (for example Ennion's gladiator beakers) and the production of true asymmetry, as in the flasks modelled to resemble bunches of grapes, human heads or animals. This type of mould blown glass opened up an original avenue of possible shapes, one that has been exploited by glassmakers and designers ever since. The way in which makers like Ennion exploited the use of simple clay moulds to produce items that reflected transitory local events (gladiator contests), and also used it to sign his work, shows originality and marketing flair. The use of steam-bent wood moulds by Alvar Aalto in the early 20th century to produce truly asymmetric blown forms was a similarly creative step, as were the bottles made by Amelung in America in the 19th century to celebrate local politicians and entertainers. Aalto's Savoy vase (see above) was through its curvilinear forms, every bit as much of a signature object as Ennion's had been, and produced in very much the same spirit.

(ABOVE) *A group of brass dip-moulds. By dipping the glass bubble into such a mould prior to its enlargement by blowing, a pattern is imprinted into the glass surface. This remains as an optical pattern in the finished object. Patterns vary, some allowing the conversion of indentations into rows of bubbles by a subsequent gather of glass trapping air in the depressions. This results in the production of an item that displays a pattern of variation within the glass wall.*
Royal Brierley Crystal Ltd. Photo, David Jones.

(RIGHT) *A decanter with a strong dip-moulded pattern in evidence. In a free-blown form such as this one, the pattern manifests itself as regular variations of surface thickness. If, however, the glass is blown into a mould to give it its final form, the dip-moulded pattern will be pushed wholly onto the interior surface, giving a totally different effect. This form of the technique is known as optic patterning.*
Broadfield House Glass Museum. Photo, David Jones.

Moulds, of course, could be (and were) used as only partial formers of the glass, with additions of hot glass gathers, and manipulation used to add details like handles and rims; the Roman pilgrim bottles shaped like shells are classic examples. Moulds can also be used to impart a partial pattern to the bubble at a very early stage, which is maintained even when it is enlarged by free or mould blowing (see opposite page, left column). This is called dip moulding, and usually creates a series of regular distortions in the disposition of the glass wall. This forms an optical pattern within the fabric of the glass (see opposite page, right column), caused by differing thicknesses, which, when used with transparent glass shows as a light-distorting pattern. Where a bubble that has been given such a pattern by the use of a dip-mould is blown into another mould to give it its final shape this distortion is, of course, enlarged and forced into the inside surface as projections, while the outside surface is flattened by contact with the mould's surface. This is called an optic, and appears to be within the glass rather than projected from the surface, as is the case with dip moulded patterns that have been free-blown.

So, within a few years of its development, glassblowing had been exploited fully, and its complete range of possibilities developed creatively. Although, during its two thousand year dominance it constantly renewed itself through the development of new variants of this range, it wasn't until pressing was invented in the 19th century that a radically new way of glassforming challenged the total domination of glassblowing systems of making (see below). In terms of invention, few procedures are entirely new, most can be described as novel extensions to traditional ways of working or more probably new juxta-positions or combinations of elements of existing

A press mould, showing the relatively simple basic procedure, even for machine production. The mould is split to allow easy removal, and the glass is pushed into the form by a vertical plunger that also forms the interior shape. Despite its relative simplicity, such moulds are expensive, well-engineered items because of their sustained use at high temperatures.
Broadfield House Glass Museum. Photo, David Jones.

processes. The basic principles, process, techniques and tools that were developed during the 1st century AD were flexible enough to respond to variations in circumstance, whether of stylistic, economic, geographic or social origin. New products emerged as each civilisation required them without creating the need for new production systems. There were, of course, improvements to individual elements of the original system, the evolution of the glassmakers chair for example, but actual additions to the basic repertoire are extremely rare. Apparently simple procedures like the addition of trails or blobs of hot glass were constantly re-interpreted by new generations of makers, and managed to yield effects that were stylistically distinct from each other, and which managed to brilliantly reflect the society they served (see p.46 and right). Another reason for glassblowing's survival and dominance over such a long historical period was that in terms of craft production it was extremely efficient, providing an effective and fast way of producing useful and decorative objects. The technology needed to make glass from its raw materials was complex in the way in which it drew influences from a variety of sources (ceramic and metal particularly) but simple in its operation, and capable of adjustment to shifting sources of fuel, materials and circumstance.

A high quality, marketable blown object could be made in a relatively short time by a skilled blower, served by a small team of less skilled workers. The main drawback in the system was its reliance on a high level of skill and the time and investment required to train workers to this level. The glassmaking team performed a useful function on both fronts, comprising a number of separate positions, each requiring a distinct increasing level of skill, from the boy who carried the finished objects to the annealing oven to the servitor who gathered the correct amounts of glass for the gaffer to work with. The team's existence removed the necessity for the gaffer to perform mundane tasks, thereby maximising the use of his skill, and at the same time provided an apprenticeship ladder within the team for those able enough to use it. Top glassblowers, despite the need for years of training, are born as much as made, and each one imparts their own particular making signature to the glass, no matter how simple or repetitive the object made. This

Three-dimensional trailing. Simple blobs of glass pulled vertically down the vessel to create organic features. Made at Whitefriars in 1930.

Broadfield House Glass Museum. Photo, David Jones.

individuality may well be behind the singular exploitation of simple techniques over the centuries. The way in which, despite the restrictions imposed on them by the practical, repetitive nature of their work, small details were made to evolve into *tours de force* that in some cases gradually came to dominate the original form. The use of the prunt in Waldglas was clearly developed from an aid to the grip on drinking vessels, but evolved stylistically into (strictly unnecessary) rows covering the form. The same is true of numerous other examples, like the incredible

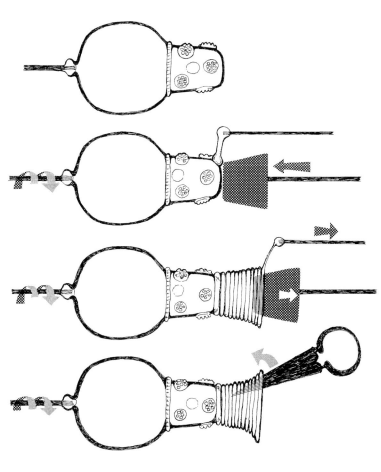

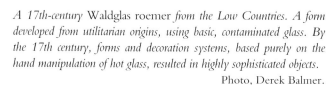

A 17th-century Waldglas roemer *from the Low Countries. A form developed from utilitarian origins, using basic, contaminated glass. By the 17th century, forms and decoration systems, based purely on the hand manipulation of hot glass, resulted in highly sophisticated objects.*
Photo, Derek Balmer.

The production of the characteristic wound, trailed foot of the Waldglas roemer. *After blowing the main body and covering it with prunts, a wooden mandrel is held against the base and a trail of glass attached to the base and wound round the mandrel by rotating the blowing iron. When formed, the mandrel is removed and the foot flared using pressure from closed shears. This technique requires a high level of skill. The* roemer *is finished by puntying (to the main body of the vessel inside the foot) and shearing the rim.*

trailed feet of the Waldglas roemer (see above and right) wound round a wooden mandrel. Both of these examples must have taken generations to evolve, with each slight change and elaboration built into an empirical system, and driven, at least partly, by the need for individual expression. Such results are, without doubt, high points in the history of glass design and making, despite the fact that they do not have a single author. It is tempting to see in such features the voice of individual creativity suppressed by the production system, and it is

certainly true in my own experience that glass gaffers working within the surviving craft based industries are justifiably proud of their individual skills, and keen to demonstrate them whenever possible. A classic example existed within the renowned Hill brothers, Charlie, Frank and Tom, who worked together at Whitefriars, London in the mid 20th century. They were all equally skilled gaffers, yet each developed a particular range of specialist glassmaking skills, and each represented the height of those skills within the factory. The precise

(ABOVE) *Detail of a vessel by George Elliott showing his use of splashes of colour, created by the application of small shards and horizontal trailing which is 'combed' with a metal spike to create the decorative effect. An example of a contemporary maker using historical techniques originally associated with anonymous functional ware in his own, distinctive, craft objects.*

Photo, Janet Elliott.

Lightbulb machine at Osram factory. The volume of bulbs required made it necessary to develop a process and machine capable of making enormous numbers at low cost. The result was the Westlake machine, designed in 1922, where a continuous ribbon of molten glass passed over a series of apertures and moulds, allowing the production of thousands of identical bulbs an hour. Here the bulbs are being sealed automatically to their metal holders. Even this aspect required the development of glass to metal compatibility.

Science Museum Picture Library, London.

nature of a making signature might be very small, particularly within a simple, functional form. The way in which essential details like rims or handles are set and given shape may be the only opportunity to impart it in a making time measured in minutes. It is a basic economic fact that the decoration or elaboration's of blown glass carried out during its actual manufacture as a hot, ductile liquid are efficient ways of adding to its value. It is the work of only a few extra minutes to add extra trailing, pincering (see left, upper picture), or dip moulding, add a few fragments of splashed colour (see opposite). This is why vernacular forms, made largely by the groups actually using them in their daily lives are invariably decorated in this way, and is in strict contrast to decoration and elaboration carried out after glass objects are cold. Processes like cutting, engraving or enamelling could, in pre-industrial times, increase the cost of an object by a factor of twenty. This would immediately transform a practical drinking vessel from an object of everyday use to one with a strong ceremonial or stylistic function. This truth is, of course, purely relative to glassmaking as a craft based, pre-industrial system. As Adam Smith pointed out, once the time taken to make an object became more expensive than its material, the scene was set for the industrialisation of making systems. In such a system the number of identical objects that can be produced within a given time, be it cars or light bulbs (see left, lower picture), becomes the major criteria by which they are judged. Even those craft based industries that managed to survive the mechanisation process, and which use individual hand-made skills as their main justification for continued existence (and high prices) have not been immune to rationalised procedures which, once adopted, have eroded the very aspect they have sought to market. A simple example from glass-making will illustrate this process; the creation of the rim of a wineglass. From the development of glassblowing in the 1st century AD until the 21st century the way in which containers were made involved transferring the bubble to a punty iron and opening out the small irregular opening made by cracking off the blowing iron. The glass was re-heated to make it soft enough to do this and in the case of some shapes, like wineglasses, the excess glass was cut away with shears and re-heated (see p.88).

A vernacular jug with 'splashed' decoration; 19th-century English. The addition of a decorative surface to this essentially practical, workaday object was the work of a few seconds of making time. The bubble of glass was rolled in fragments of coloured glass spread on the marver. A minimum of effort for a maximum effect.
Broadfield House Glass Museum. Photo, David Jones.

The Embassy Suite made by Frank Hill and designed by H. Powell at Whitefriars in 1938. A main characteristic of this handmade suite of wineglasses is its delicate organic sheared rim. The addition of such detailing requires both time and extreme skill, and is an increasingly rare feature of hand-blown production.
The Museum of London.

This created a soft and aesthetically beautiful rim to the glass that was also comfortable to drink from. Unfortunately, the creation of such a rim was found to be, in 20th-century terms, too expensive in its use of time and human skill, even within an industry that marketed the craft nature of its products. A procedure was invented that did away with both the need to transfer the bubble to the punty iron and to shear the excess glass, thus speeding up the process. The bowl was blown into a turn round mould, and the stem and foot added while still attached to the iron. This whole form was then cracked away from the iron and cooled. After cooling the excess glass was removed by semi-automatic means and a rim created by softening in a concentrated flame (see opposite). While the bead created by this means is a perfectly adequate solution, it lacks the organic feel of the genuine hand crafted original. The irony behind this illustration is two-fold. The survival of glassblowing as the dominant method for working

glass was due in the main to its efficiency in economic terms, it was only the industrial revolution that altered the equation and left the craft based industries in general, outside the mass produced mainstream. The other irony is that in order to survive, such industries had to stress their individual, hand crafted ethos (and the higher prices that resulted) at the same time as seeking ways of bypassing as much of this as possible.

The difficulties experienced by glassblowing as a factory based system in the 20th century were circumvented by the glass studio. Studios are smaller, centred round named designer makers, and aggressively market both the hand crafted nature of their products and also their status as sources of signature objects. From being for most of its history a supremely anonymous process, glassblowing, as practised by studio makers, boasts the best known glass makers of any glass process. Makers such as Dale Chihuly and Erwin Eisch project and market their

(TOP) *The creation of a rim without either puntying or shearing. The glass is blown in one stage, leaving an 'overblow' of excess glass. This is removed by a 'cracking off' machine to leave a sharp edge.*

Royal Brierley Crystal Ltd. Photo, David Jones.

(ABOVE) *The final stage, after cracking the excess off, the rim area is melted to create a soft bead of glass round the rim. This is acceptable as a drinking surface and is, of course, quicker and cheaper than shearing, but does not match its aesthetic quality.*

Royal Brierley Crystal Ltd. Photo, David Jones.

productions as art works, and through the intensely visual nature of their hot glass making, themselves as performers. The objects that emerge from this use of glass as a creative medium are viewed, collected, valued and discussed in terms that used to be the preserve of fine art. Much of the character of this perception of a process, which has been associated with the production of useful containers for most of its existence, derives from the personal nature of the relationship between maker and material. It is a phenomenon that has developed only within the last few decades and of course is part of the wider re-positioning of craft activities in general that has taken place since 1945. It could only have taken place within a cultural system that values the signature of the artist so highly, particularly where each work displays its individual nature within its forms, effects, colours and textures. It is a characteristic of the modern glass movement that its studio produced objects are recognised as being by a named maker without recourse to the actual signature on them. This is a revolution in perception and use, and although it has been brought about by economic and social forces, it has been made possible by the nature of the material and by the way in which studio glass has combined designing and making within a single individual. This is distinct from the other characteristic of our own era, the named designer who decides the form but does not make the object. It is, for instance Phillip Webb the architect we acknowledge as the author of the glass for William Morris, not the unknown glassmaker who carried out his designs using traced profiles and callipers to ensure the accurate interpretation of the design drawing.

FLAT GLASS

None of this could have occurred without the shift that began with the search for a better method of flat glass manufacture in the late 17th century, and which led eventually to the industrialised production of the vast majority of glass products. An account of the mechanisation of glass production is necessarily dominated by the individuals who had the vision and ingenuity to develop the new approaches to the material that made the new processes possible. This centred on the shaping of glass into large numbers of identical objects without recourse to traditional (slow and expensive) hand skills. Two distinct ways of doing this emerged: one developed entirely new production methods, e.g. sheet rolling, while the other copied the separate stages of hand production within specially designed machine systems. This enabled pioneers like Perrot to disengage from traditional thinking and re-state the problem of flat glass manufacture in new and separate terms.

It is important to make a distinction between window and mirror glass. Sheet glass for windows was made well within the glassblowing system. The traditional cylinder and crown methods produced panes of reasonable quality and cost well into the 19th century (the cylinder method is illustrated on pp91 and 92, and the crown method in the first two illustrations on p.93). It was the demand for sheet glass capable of being ground and polished into mirrors of quality and scale, to grace the large neo-classical houses of the rich, that created the imperative for a new flat glass method. To be capable of acting as mirrors the glass had to be produced thick enough to allow it to be ground and polished on both sides to achieve a uniform thickness prior to silvering (actually thin lead foil). Sheet glass produced by cylinder or crown is too thin to allow for such grinding, and is too irregular to function as

an effective mirror. Windows in old houses that still have their original glass can be seen to have originated from these craft processes by virtue of their irregularities. It is often possible to see clearly whether they have been produced by the cylinder (ripples across) or crown (radial). In order to produce sheet glass thick enough to allow grinding it had to be produced by direct casting from gathering irons or ladles, and this only produced extremely small sheets, and caused mirrors to be rare, costly, and small.

Perrot's solution was to devise a system that involved a larger amount of liquid glass and to deliver it in a more appropriate form for the production of rectangular sheets. All glassblowing procedures are predicated on the central nature of the blowing and gathering iron. As usual with the mechanisation of glass production, the area requiring the greatest degree of originality was the point and nature of the delivery of the hot glass. This was because of the special nature and behaviour of the hot glass at that point, and the extent to which it dominated the process

(PP 91–2)
Production of sheet glass by the cylinder method at Chance Brothers in 1920. By this time, this method, which had been used to produce all of the glass for the Crystal Palace in 1851, was only used to make specialist sheet glass for stained glass. The process illustrated is, however, essentially the same as that employed for over a thousand years to make window glass. The only real difference being the gantry supports that lifted and moved the cylinder. This system enabled the production of much larger cylinders than by manual means alone.

(P.91, TOP) *Building the necessary weight of glass on the blowing iron. The accumulation of enough glass to produce a 1.8 m (6 ft) cylinder had to be done in stages, with each gather being allowed to cool and stiffen slightly before the addition of the next. The glassmakers are rotating the irons over a trough of water which they scoop up and douse the iron to keep it cool.*

(P.91, INSET) *The completed gather of glass is partly formed by rotation into a floor-mounted depression while air is blown down the iron to further inflate it. Even at this stage the operation requires two men.*

(P.91, BOTTOM) *The form is elongated by swinging the bubble into a pit while the iron is supported on a rig that is hung from an overhead gantry.*

All photos from Pilkington Bros Ltd Archive.

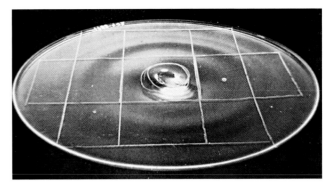

A typical crown. The pattern of panes has been marked on it, showing the distortion in thickness across each pane, the amount of waste, and the central bullseye section traditionally used in the least important buildings, but now much sought after.

Pilkington Bros Ltd Archive.

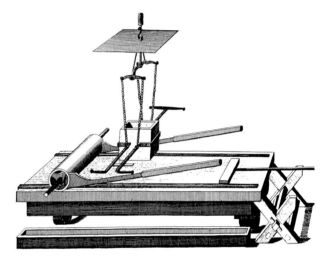

The production of sheet glass by the crown method. Spinning a bubble of glass that has been puntied, sheared and opened up to create a circle of flattish glass. Note the half wall and face and eye protection provided by metal mesh sections on stands. Sometimes similar sections were hung round the neck on strings and held in front of the face by a wooden peg clamped between the teeth, while the glassmaker was exposed to the furnace heat.

Pilkington Bros Ltd Archive.

The plate glass system developed in the late-17th century. This was a radically new approach to the casting of large sheets of glass for mirrors. It comprised a copper-topped table with guide runners to contain and determine the thickness of the glass. Hot liquid glass was poured on to it from a ceramic container that had been dipped into the furnace, and a roller was pulled across the glass to spread it. Although this process was subject to constant refinement, improvement and extension during subsequent centuries, the original break with tradition remains the most important.

(OPPOSITE PAGE)

(TOP) *The end of the cylinder is opened up.*

(BELOW) *The finished cylinder is moved from the blowing shop to the annealing lehr by use of the counterbalanced rig that runs along wires.*

Both photos Pilkington Bros Ltd Archive.

determined its success or failure. Perrot's initial solution was a rectangular box, which was dipped into the furnace to fill it with enough molten glass to cast a large sheet, and to move this, suspended on chains, across a table made of copper followed by a hand drawn roller (see the pictures above and the top illustrations on p.94). The glass lost precious heat in its move from furnace to table and in its pouring from the tilted ceramic crucible (cuvette).

(RIGHT) *Plate casting in the 1930s. Despite the fact that 250 years separate this from the previous illustration, the process is almost identical. Only the scale has changed. Plate glass for mirrors and architectural use was cast by this method and then ground and polished by a complex process involving the setting of the plates on to a soft surface by hand and their polishing with a rotary series of heads. This continued until the invention of the float process.*

Pilkington Bros Ltd Archive.

(BELOW) *One of the massive tank furnaces built in the 1950s to produce float glass. The development of the tank furnace in the 19th century, whereby large quantities of glass were continuously produced, was an essential element in the manufacture of glass objects on a large scale. Raw batch was fed into one end of the tank and founded glass drawn off at the other, thereby eliminating the gap between filling pots and working them.*

Both photos Pilkington Bros Ltd Archive.

CASTING THE GLASS

This picture shows the molten glass being poured on the casting table. The overhead crane empties the crucible along the table in front of the roller.

Casting the Glass

The casting table is hollow, water-cooled and made of iron, and at one end lies a great roller covering its whole width.

The molten glass is poured out upon the table and the roller slowly moves (just once) across it, flattening it into a broad plate.

Adjustable gauges at the sides of the table regulate the thickness of the plate.

The glass soon loses its white-hot glow and becomes greenish-white in colour, translucent but not transparent. Its surface is rough, coarse, and unpromising, but inside it is crystal clear. Any sudden exposure to cold air would crack it, so most elaborate precautions have to be taken to ensure gradual cooling.

A Colburn sheet drawing machine. Irving W. Colburn started experiments with sheet drawing in 1900 but the machine was not perfected until 1913 when it went into production. The glass was founded in a tank furnace (to the right in the photograph) and drawn from a reservoir using a bait dipped in the glass. As the sheet was drawn up vertically it was gripped and shaped by a pair of channelled rollers at the edges of the sheet. When the sheet had risen a few feet it was softened by gas jets and bent horizontally. The process was still in use in the 1950s.
Ward Canaday Centre, University of Toledo, USA.

As with all successful mechanisation processes, in glass it was subject to many improvements over the next two centuries. The cuvette was replaced by a tilting furnace; tables and rollers became mechanised as new sources of power (steam and then electricity) became available. The sheets of glass it was capable of producing became larger and of better quality, to the point where the product replaced cylinder and crown glass for windows in the late 19th century. To my mind, none of the improvements match the initial original thinking of the early pioneers and it is amazing that glass for mirrors and large scale architectural plate glass still required grinding and polishing over its entire surface until the invention of the radical float glass process in the 1960s.

Other inventive individuals developed continuous flat glass production systems, made possible by the new, large, efficient furnaces and power sources available by the end of the 19th century (see previous page, bottom picture). These processes, which eventually allowed the production of continuously drawn sheet, cylinder and tube, although totally new in concept and design were still based on the exploitation of the unique properties of glass. These processes exploited the innate sticky, elastic nature of the material by using specially shaped ceramic forms to dip into and adhere to the glass. The molten mass, at its point of contact with the ceramic bait was given its initial form by the way it adhered to it and the glass was drawn from or through the static or moving bait (see above). Using new technology, temperature controls and power sources a large tank of liquid

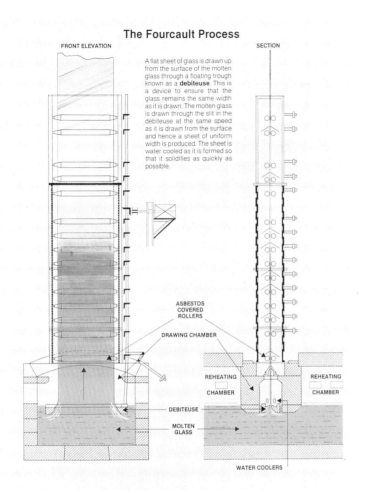

The Fourcault Process

FRONT ELEVATION **SECTION**

A flat sheet of glass is drawn up from the surface of the molten glass through a floating trough known as a **debiteuse**. This is a device to ensure that the glass remains the same width as it is drawn. The molten glass is drawn through the slit in the debiteuse at the same speed as it is drawn from the surface and hence a sheet of uniform width is produced. The sheet is water cooled as it is formed so that it solidifies as quickly as possible.

ASBESTOS COVERED ROLLERS

DRAWING CHAMBER

REHEATING CHAMBER   REHEATING CHAMBER

DEBITEUSE

MOLTEN GLASS

WATER COOLERS

A diagram of the Fourcault process. Like all automated processes it relied on a precise equilibrium existing between all of the aspects of the process. The slightest change in any one of the forces involved would cause the system to break down. For example, the debiteuse was prone to erosion through prolonged contact with hot glass, causing the glass sheet to become marked with linear distortions.

Science Museum Picture Library, London.

The main liquid container of the 18th century: the green bottle. Free blown in large quantities in dark, contaminated glass. Specialist bottle furnaces had to be developed to produce enough glass to cope with the demand for them.

Broadfield House Glass Museum. Photo, David Jones.

glass could be drawn off in the form of sheet or cylinders. These processes needed many years of dedication to perfect, and required the solution of many problems, often related to the nature of liquid glass. For example, sheet drawn by the Fourcault process (see above, left) was prone to the fault of waisting, where the sheet narrowed in width as it was pulled upwards. This reduced both the width and consistency of the product. The problem was solved by the use of compressed air blowers positioned to cool the edges of the sheet and harden them. Such systems rely on the establishment of an equilibrium of the forces involved, to ensure their repeatability. As long as this equilibrium is maintained, the product is the inevitable result of its continued operation. If any of the aspects of the system vary by only a small amount, the whole

operation is at risk. This makes their daily, trouble free operation amazing given the fact that they take as their starting point the organic, mobile viscous material of glass.

Where mechanisation aimed to provide the same basic products as blowing but simply wanted to make them cheaper and in larger quantities, a different kind of enquiry ensued. Glassblowing was a supremely efficient method of container production, which is why it dominated for so long, but, by the late 19th century demand was great, and labour costs had risen to a point where some method of mechanisation was essential. In terms of quantity the bottle (see above, right) offered the most profitable glass container to mechanise, with the added advantage that by using such methods the products could be standardised to a degree not possible by the

(LEFT) *A hand-operated bottle neck former. The bottle would be free-blown, puntied, and the neck area softened in the furnace mouth. This would be placed over the central screw former and the two handles pushed together, creating a screw thread on the inside of the bottle neck (requiring it to be unscrewed quickly from the device) and shape the outside of the bottle neck. Mechanisation was the result of numbers of smaller steps such as this one in the late 19th century.*

Royal Brierley Crystal Ltd. Photo, David Jones.

(BELOW LEFT) *The bottle furnace. A large structure that contained numbers of open pots. These were raised up above the burning coal, and the heat brought into the pot chamber through an iron grating. The contaminated nature of the bottle glass meant that open pots could be used, even with coal.*

Pilkington Bros Ltd Archive.

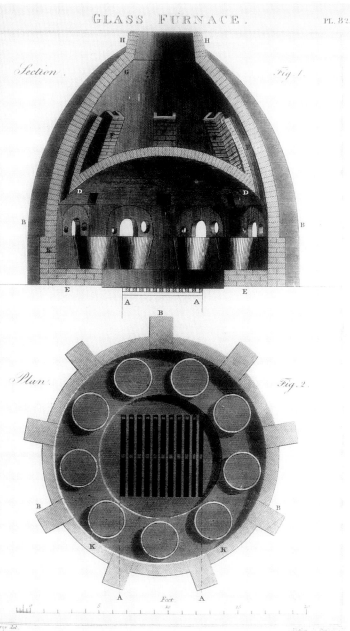

use of traditional skills. This was particularly desirable in an era where products increasingly relied on the shape of the container as an integral part of its marketing identity. Joseph Schweppe was manufacturing mineral water in Bristol by 1794 and in the late 19th century products like *Coca Cola* had become synonymous with their distinctive containers. The new methods of manufacture, by their break with craft production techniques, made it possible to standardise bottles and jars at the same time as giving them their distinctive shapes, names and trademarks.

Totally new systems such as flat glass casting and the standardisation and mechanisation of bottle-making, were achieved slowly, by breaking down the hand procedures into their separate parts (see above, left) and addressing each as a discrete problem. The full mechanisation took many decades, partly because essential parts of the equation were initially missing, like new forms of motive power or compressed air, and partly because some problems were so difficult to solve (see left and overleaf, left column).

It is entirely fitting that this original aspect of glass development occurred in America in the 19th and early 20th centuries. The development of new, machine based processes for glass was part of a wider approach to production systems in general, from Samuel Colt to Henry Ford. All of the forces necessary came together: need, means and motive. As usual, important advances in glass design and technology happened within an optimistic, expanding culture, with an appropriate economy

The glass cone, developed in England to create the updraught necessary to reach the high temperature needed to burn coal.

Pilkington Bros Ltd Archive.

An Ashley glass bottle. Made by a machine invented by the Englishman Howard Ashley. Ashley obtained a patent for a bottlemaking machine in 1886 but it took him another three years to come up with a practical method of producing narrow-necked bottles such as this one. His three-stage process dictated the design of the semi-automatic system. Crucially the machine still relied on a skilled glassmaker to feed it with the accurate gathers of hot glass.

Science Museum Picture Library, London.

and scientific attitude. Perhaps more important than any of these, however, was the way in which this mix encouraged the emergence of the dynamic individual, often self-trained, who was able to disengage their creative thinking from past methods.

Bottle-making naturally retained the principle of inflation, eventually substituting compressed air for lung power, and initially sought to improve both production and product by the use of moulds. Within this aspect of the process two problems existed: body and neck. These were addressed by the use of complex split metal moulds and the

development of devices that combined the blowing iron with a plunger to form the neck as the bottle was blown. Starting as early as 1821 this line of invention led to sophisticated systems capable of forming a complete bottle, without any hand finishing, in one session. Patents were granted for such devices from the 1860s to 1880s. Although these were ground breaking advances, particularly the way in which they reversed the old hand system by forming the neck shape first and then inflating it into a mould, they were still totally reliant on two residues of the past: hand gathering and blowing. Both of these needed skill, and succeeded more because of the way in which they could deliver a standardised product than their efficiency in terms of speed (see above). Although the workforce required was less skilled, an early machine (the Ashley) still needed seven workers to operate it. These early devices ('machine' is less appropriate because of their reliance on hand gathering and blowing) contained two new design elements that were essential for the development of fully automated systems. This created a two stage process which became press and blow or blow and blow; it did this by separating the creation of an initial bubble from its inflation into a finished container. It was achieved either by pressing into the

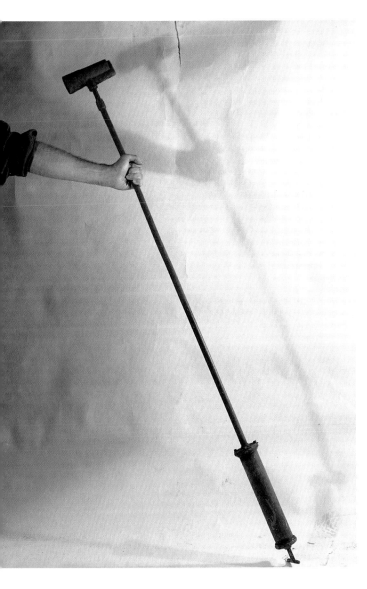

A hand-operated gathering device, operating on the same principle as that devised by Michael Owens for his bottle-making machine. The plunger is pulled out, sucking hot glass into the cup. The shaped gather of glass is then delivered to a mould by pushing the plunger in.

Royal Brierley Crystal Ltd. Photo, David Jones.

gob of glass or by blowing air into it. Once this pre-shape was formed the glass was moved to a larger mould for full inflation. In order to form the neck of the bottle first, it was necessary to also create a partly shaped bubble, extending from the neck pressing device that held and shaped the initial gather of glass. This involved producing a bubble as part of the initial gather which was fully inflated when introduced into the mould. This was achieved by one of two methods: press, pushing a plunger into the

glass mass, or blowing down the iron through the neck forming device. This pre-formed shape was transferred to a mould and inflated to make the complete bottle. The system became known as either press and blow or blow and blow and formed the models for fully automated systems capable of producing millions of bottles or jars a day. By 1917 Americans O'Neill and Lynch managed to automate blowing and mould systems, calling their system 'no-boy', to draw attention to this advance, but they still needed to be fed by a skilled gatherer. There were many different machines based on the same principles and subject to the same drawback, for despite their advances they could still only manage to produce two hundred bottles per hour. There were many attempts to solve the problem of automatic feeding, including filling moulds from a stream of molten glass, which was difficult to control as it needed to be sheared, and bubbles became trapped in the glass mass by the folding action of the glass flow. In practice the delivery of a pre-shaped gob of molten glass capable of inflation into a bottle proved to be the most intractable of the problems associated with the new system. It required the inspired efforts of two different individuals to solve the problem, and although both came up with different but successful solutions they both had to come to terms with the nature of glass, and to start from a rich traditional viewpoint. Michael Owens, a largely self-taught engineer from Ohio was the first to solve this problem, although it took him many years of trial and error, even though his principle of gathering the right amount of glass through suction remained the same. His solution and its incorporation into a fully automatic machine by 1903 was acclaimed as 'one of the most brilliant inventions in the history of inventions' whose 'methods had nothing in common with those of other inventors'.[22] His first 'A type' machine had an output capacity of 18000 bottles (see overleaf) in 24 hours with labour costs reduced to one tenth of the semi-automatics (see left). His principle of gathering by suction required a stiffer, less viscous glass than that used for hand making. This illustrates an important factor governing machine processes, the more specific the process the more specific its requirements in terms of temperature, glass composition and consistency. Hand driven craft systems allow for considerable

Michael Owens's experimental bottle former. Although this early device was not successful it nevertheless established the principles that were essential for the later fully automatic machines. The device sucks up the required amount of glass from a ladle, pre-shapes it, and blows it into a bottle by use of the plunger. Crude though this appears, it was a radical and creative departure from traditional methods.

Science Museum Picture Library, London.

variations to be accommodated by the skill of the craftsperson.

Owens's machines were closed systems, in the sense that they could only be purchased complete, they could not cope with demand and there was still a need for an automatic feeder system capable of converting the hand-fed semi-automatic systems. Dr Karl Peiler developed a system called the Hartford

paddle feeder which relied on a moving paddle to displace a shaped gob of glass into the machine. By 1922 this had evolved into the single feeder version which used a shaped plunger passing through a molten stream of glass to expel pre-shaped gobs of glass into the machine (see opposite page, top right).

Within the development of a complex system many sub-problems have to be solved. An example being Owens's need to present his suction gathering device to a different part of the surface of the molten glass each time to avoid chilling. This he solved, after years of experiment, by rotating the furnace itself between each suction gather. The individual section machine, developed in 1925, avoided the problems involved in the rotation of large numbers of moulds by keeping the moulds static, (see opposite, top left) and instead of delivering gobs of molten glass to them. Solutions and improvements to these early systems meant that each new generation of machines outdid their predecessors with dramatic increases in yield and product quality (see opposite, bottom photograph). Nevertheless it is important to distinguish between a better way of carrying out an established process and the establishment of its principles in the first place. The originality of Michael Owens was considerable and many-layered, but relied ultimately on the way in which he addressed the nature of an age-old viscous material that was radically new, and, through creativity and patient experiment found a way of making it compatible with the same kind of 20th-century production systems that were being devised to form advanced metal alloys and plastics.

(OPPOSITE PAGE)

(ABOVE LEFT) *A single mould, or station, from a bottle-making machine. The only real difference between this and a traditional, non-mechanised mould, is in the sophisticated cooling system and the automated operation.*

(ABOVE RIGHT) *Shaped gobs of hot glass being delivered into bottle stations. The glass is formed by the Hartford feeder system where a plunger pushes hot glass through an aperture to create this form. Coolant can be seen, ensuring that the precise temperatures for all parts of the process are maintained.*

(BELOW) *A multi-station machine showing the completed bottles emerging from the individual mould stations onto the conveyor belt taking them to the lehr for cooling.*

All photos British Glass Manufacturers' Federation.

CHAPTER FOUR

Chronology

'Until the advent of the scientific age, technological advances were based on craft experience,
and the personal element in transmitting such experience from one generation to another, and
from one place to another, was exceptionally strong.'
A. R. J. P. Ubbelohde, *History of Technology*, Vol. IV, Oxford, 1958.

'Culture is a compost in which many traits temporarily disappear or become
unidentifiable, but few are ever lost.'
Lewis Mumford.

At first glance any attempt to ascribe a strict chronological progression to the history of glassmaking and forming appears to contradict a major tenet of this book. I have been at pains to describe my belief that each succeeding civilisation re-interpreted glass as a material in its own image, to the extent that often only the basic material, glass remained. All other aspects, products, processes, values, functions and aesthetic preferences shifted emphasis, often dramatically. Nevertheless, there is a profound difference between constant re-interpretation and constant re-discovery, for re-interpretation carries with it an implication of continuity within the changing uses of glass by successive civilisations and cultures. As Samuel Kurinsky puts it, 'Glassmaking is unique among the arts, in that the process seems to have been invented only once in all of human history'.[23] If this is true then indeed its mysteries must have been handed down an unbroken line of succession from 3000 BC to the present day.

THE FIRST GLASS

When I first started studying glass in the early 1960s the date of its first manifestation was fixed firmly within the 15th century BC during the reign of Thutmose III. This was associated with a particular core-formed vessel that bears his cartouche, and

illustrates the dangerous tendency to base observations on the accidental survival of objects. From this, inferences were drawn that glass was a discovery of the Egyptian civilisation and, therefore, the processes of core-forming and mosaic-fusion were essentially Egyptian too. All of these assumptions were wrong, and I mention them in the expectation that events, discoveries and scholarship will in turn force further reassessments of our current, partial understanding. I have often used the terms cuckoo and chameleon to describe the nature of glass, its development, and its use as a material. The sophisticated technology needed to sustain glass manufacture derives from a variety of allied material technologies, predominantly ceramic and metal. These are needed to provide heat sources, tools, furnaces, and material science, and as such need to pre-date the use of glass within a society. Glass, therefore, does not usually emerge until a culture is well established, when it can take whatever it requires for its own development. By the time this happens the formal languages used to give shapes to ceramic, metal and wood are usually well established, so that glass objects emerge against the background of strong traditions of shape and decoration. As a result, glass objects invariably begin their life within a society by copying forms and styles from those used by other materials. However, despite this chameleon behaviour (which is common throughout its history) one of the fascinating things about glass is the way in which it rapidly usurps its borrowed forms, by their shift into this unique material and its making systems. Time and again, despite inheriting powerful original shapes from ceramic, metal and stone, they were rapidly transformed into essentially 'glassy' forms. This can often be seen at its best in small details, and the way in which the maker has reinterpreted the original to suit the material, and its tools and processes, through the development of creative, physical skills. A handle which derived from ceramic, and which was appropriate to the use of a coil of hand manipulated clay, became, when adopted by glassmakers, a sinuous liquid arabesque that derived from the essential nature of a trail of cooling glass shaped by hand held metal tools. The truly surprising aspect of such developments was how quickly they occurred whenever they were needed. Glass may often be a latecomer to the party but it rapidly makes its presence felt.

These two characteristics go some way to explain why glass can often be used in such contradictory ways by societies that follow one another chronologically. Another reason is its neutrality in terms of material value, i.e. its inherent worth is not determined by its status, like gold or silver. Rather it relates to rarity, time and skill, and above all to the objects and materials it is associated with. Where glass is formed by goldsmiths into similar forms, its value is equally high, but when it is produced in quantity into shapes that work alongside more mundane materials it, chameleon-like, takes its status from them. A major 20th century dictum was Louis Sullivan's 'form follows function' although it has often been used to mean 'form follows ease of manufacture'. It is certainly true that the chronological development of some materials do display a linear development which includes an incremental progression towards greater production speed and efficiency. The history of glass contains aspects of this, but, taken as a whole, it cannot be understood in these terms. Certainly the Victorians, for whom such progress was an axiom of their society, found it impossible to judge objects like core-formed vessels except as inefficient by comparison with blown equivalents. As a result it was not until 1940 that the first book was published about ancient glass which accepted its relevance to a different context.[24] Despite the obvious fact that the history of glass does demonstrate a coherent chronology (otherwise it would have to have been constantly reinvented by each new user) it is neither incremental or progressive. An analogy might be of a relay race in which each recipient of the baton reshapes it to his/her personal specification before eventually handing it on. Also, in such a race each lap would be run at a different speed and the baton might even be passed sideways to participants in a different race instead of constantly forward. This is probably labouring the point but it is worth stressing that, within a traceable continuity, there are many apparent contradictions throughout five thousand years of development.

At the moment it is possible to follow glass back to a supposed source in the Bronze Age, about 3000 years BC. It seems unlikely that it could have developed much before this, because of its requirements in technological terms. Glass is a synthetic and was the first to be developed by humankind. This in itself was a sophisticated concept for a culture that was used to using materials that were already in existence, wood, bone and stone or refining or altering naturally occurring substances, metal and clay. Glass in contrast, was the result of combining a mixture of unlikely materials through heat, and its emergence as a synthesised

SOME MILESTONES
IN THE HISTORY OF GLASS
Broadly they represent three important threads within its development.

MATERIAL:
techniques/processes/devices/machines

OBJECTS:
forms/functions/style

CONTEXT:
political/social/economic/geographic

5000 BC	GLAZED STEATITE
5000 BC	FAIENCE PRODUCTION
2600 BC	EXISTENCE OF 'EGYPTIAN BLUE'
2100 BC	FAIENCE PRODUCTION BY CEMENTATION
2000 BC	FIRST INDICATIONS OF GLASS AS AN INDEPENDENT MATERIAL
1700 BC	FULL RANGE OF FAIENCE PRODUCTION
1500 BC	FIRST CORE-VESSELS IN MESOPOTAMIA
1500 BC	FLOWERING OF GLASS UNDER THUTMOSE III BEAD AND CORE FORMING
1400 BC	SHIPWRECK AT ULU BURUN. GLASS INGOTS INDICATE A TRADE IN GLASS AS A RAW MATERIAL
1400 BC	PRESSED GLASS JEWELS USING CARVED STONE MOULDS
1400 BC	FIRST CUNIEFORM TABLETS
1400 BC	TELL-EL-ARMARNA. HUGE GLASS WORKSHOPS BUILT IN THE REIGN OF AKENHATEN
1200 BC	DECLINE OF EGYPTIAN GLASS INDUSTRY
900 BC	REVIVAL OF GLASS INDUSTRY IN SYRIA AND MESOPOTAMIA
800 BC	SYRIAN SINGLE-COLOUR SLUMPED BOWLS
700 BC	SARGON VASE-CAST
600 BC	GORDION OMPHALOS-CAST
500 BC	PERSIAN CAST BOWLS
400 BC	PHIDIAS WORKSHOPS. LARGE-SCALE GLASS SLUMPING
332 BC	ESTABLISHMENT OF ALEXANDRIA AS GLASS MAKING CENTRE
330 BC	FALL OF PERSIAN EMPIRE
250 BC	MOSAIC GLASS FUSION. *MILLEFIORE* AND *RETICELLI* BOWLS
200 BC	FINAL FLOWERING OF MEDITERRANEAN CORE-FORMING INDUSTRY

material in its own right must have been a long and experimental process, whatever Pliny says about its origin as the result of a spontaneous accident.[25] The first glass was probably developed in the Mitannian or Hurrian region of Mesopotamia as an extension to the use of glazes or faience production. Both glaze and faience move from a premise of achieving a covering of glass-like coating on to a core of another material whether stone, ceramic or quartz. The first objects that involved the use of glass in their production were beads, plaques, inlays, and eventually small vessels. The Mesopotamian civilisation that emerged in the region gave a boost to the development of glass, and because they developed a written language (cuneiform) we have a record of the way in which they used it, and their attitudes to it, even if we have little in the way of actual glass from this period. These records, which were deemed to be important enough to find themselves in the Royal Library of Assurbanipal at Nineveh in the 7th century BC show that glass was seen as a material that could be made to imitate semi-precious stones (see right). This starting point established an association for glass that was to stay with it until the break up of the Ancient World. It became a material whose value derived from these associations, being accorded a status equal to that of the precious materials it imitated. Knowledge of glass making was transmitted through trade and dynastic alliances to Egypt where it took root and developed in ways that continued the path established for the material by the Mesopotamians. Only when the Egyptians produced glass did circumstances allow for complete examples to survive to the present day. Their use of glass as a material from which to form small, precious, symbolic objects of great surface richness (often opaque) was established by its first users. It was a viewpoint that was expanded and not seriously challenged until the Achaemenid Persians in the 5th century BC, and then only in terms of the language of the material rather than its value. This was part of the Iron Age revival of culture that followed the period of devastation between 1200 and 1000 BC. The revival in glass occurred in Egypt and gradually saw glass production move to new centres, many of which subtly introduced local variations of the established processes while adding some new ones. A

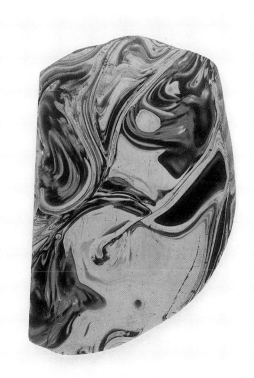

A fragment of poured, multi-coloured glass from about 100 BC. The creation of this type of glass was deliberate, and reflected the use of the material as an equivalent of natural hard stones, prized for their internal patterns.

British Museum, London.

major change was a shift in emphasis toward clear glass, particularly the Persian cast bowls, but also the single colour slumped vessels produced in Syrian workshops. This move toward clear and translucent coloured glass was as much to do with a shift of viewpoint as with any improvement in technology. As Douglas and Frank put it, 'Egyptian and Roman glass had essentially the same composition as modern soda-lime-silica-glasses',[26] and colouring clear glass was basically the same as colouring opaque. The range of colours was fairly narrow and basic, involving the addition of compounds of readily available metals, many of which were worked alongside glass. These included copper and cobalt (blues and greens), iron (green), manganese (purple), cuprous oxide (opaque red), antimony (white), lead and antimony (yellow). The fact that glass was founded from its raw materials in a simple furnace in open ceramic pots meant that colouring agents burned away in the oxygen rich fierce atmosphere created, and as a result only strong, natural materials could survive, producing a limited palette of colours. It was not until the development of the

The closed pot. Devised to counteract the contaminants caused by coal, and unwittingly providing the right circumstances for the production of full lead crystal.

Royal Brierley Crystal Ltd. Photo, David Jones.

A furnace front with the entrance to the glass pot closed by a ceramic cover. When access to the glass is required this is removed. Note the skimmer to the right of the furnace. This is used to draw across the surface of the glass before gathering.

Royal Brierley Crystal Ltd. Photo, David Jones.

closed pot (see above, left and right) in the 17th century with its more protected founding conditions that a greater range of colourants could be used and colours created, including those that required a reducing atmosphere. However the cuneiform tablets already mentioned reveal that the early glassmakers were aware of this, and actually used closed crucibles to produce small quantities of special colours.[27] The glass workshops that the Persians established by the 5th century BC were probably exclusive, producing exquisite pieces only for a ruling elite. The proximity of goldsmithing is indicated by the forms of the few surviving objects and by the probable use of lost-wax casting to make them. In addition to challenging the traditional view of glass that had been established by the Egyptians,

this created a new glass centre in the Middle East, one that was to flourish for over two thousand years and eventually play an important part in the development of Venetian glass during the Renaissance. With the gradual break up of the Egyptian civilisation, glass began to adapt to serve new masters. Military conquest and trade meant that glass objects were produced for the purposes of trade and commerce in addition to its original elite, symbolic functions. This, of course, had its impact on processes, numbers and style. The conquests of Phillip II of Macedonia and his son Alexander unified the whole area by 337 BC; on Alexander's death it was divided into four separate but still Hellenistic Kingdoms, Egypt, Syria, Mesopotamia, Greece and Macedonia. This created the conditions that gave birth to the modern order, ushered in by 30 BC when the entire Mediterranean basin was united under the Roman rule of Augustus. This created a large, unified area, which contained a number of different civilisations; their distinct traditions resulted in varied goods, which were traded across this vast region. As Ubbelohde puts it, 'High level craft skills required centres of culture, and the greater the culture the higher and more complex the spread of skills. The technological consequences of the Roman Empire, and the *Pax Romana*, spread over considerable portions of the world'. After a period, during which the techniques and processes that had served the Ancient World were given a boost by increased demand, the pressures created by this demand also caused their demise. While cast, mosaic and slumped glass were adapted to serve domestic, secular and decorative ends, their slow one-off methods meant that a process capable of large scale manufacture was required. These needs created the circumstances that gave birth to the revolutionary process of glass blowing. The cultural and economic divides that separated the ancient and modern (Roman) worlds were massive. Glass bridged those divides but only at the cost of a total transformation across its entire range of material qualities, forming methods and repertoire of object types. So dramatic was this, that it is hard to identify any aspects of ancient glass that survived beyond the 2nd century AD The fact that glass as a material did survive, and that it adapted to, and served the needs of a new system, illustrates its strange nature particularly the way in which its essential 'glassiness' could absorb, imitate, and supplant the technical and stylistic aspects of other materials.

In the Ancient World the various glass making stages had been separate, and in many cases its distinct glass procedures can be seen as offshoots of those associated with other materials. Casting, fusing, slumping and grinding are related to metalworking, ceramic and lapidary traditions. With the Romans and their exploitation of the Syrian invention of blowing, a totally new, glass-centred, system emerged, which, although it was created primarily for the practical, mass production of glass-ware also established a new tradition for the material.

In glassblowing the nature of the glass furnace, in which the ingredients are founded and the hot glass drawn off by the glassmakers, dictates the design of the system of which it is a central part. Once the ceramic pot full of glass batch and cullet has been established, and has reached founding heat it must be maintained at a high temperature, and be subject to the minimum of disturbance. This fact created the conditions that brought into being the first centralised factory system in any material. This, in turn, meant the development of a production system round the static semi-permanent nature of the furnace. In this system the raw materials from which glass was melted came into the factory and finished objects, ready for use, emerged from it. The needs of the furnace can be demonstrated by the way in which broken ceramic pots were replaced. Glass is an extremely corrosive material when hot, and the ceramic containers have a strictly finite life; when the ceramic deteriorates to the point where debris from it starts to contaminate the glass or, more spectacularly, splits, it has to be replaced. To minimise the damage to production this has to happen while the furnace is kept at a high temperature. This involves a complex and dangerous manoeuvre whereby the old pot is removed and a new one installed (set) by a team of workers clad in water-soaked clothing, and using a specially developed device. This centralisation was not just an efficient use of technology, it also had a profound impact on both the process and the objects made from it. The establishment of a factory system centred (literally) round the continuous provision of large amounts of hot glass, created a making system that was dependent on it to such an extent that very soon all glass objects were made within such factories. Processes that had been in existence for millennia died out as quickly as the cultures they had served so well. Such was the dominance of glassblowing and its factory system that even glass items that were unsuited to its inherent limitations, e.g. sheets of glass suitable for mirrors, were made within it (another cuckoo-like characteristic). Soon after its development, glassmaking by blowing began exercising a virtual monopoly of production which it operated for almost two thousand years. Even today, long after it has become an anomaly within a mechanised world, it still exerts its influence by the stereotypes of glass it has created. Our view of glass as a predominantly fragile, transparent material for containers, still dominates.

Blowing developed as a team process which revolved round the central figure of the skilled glassmaker or 'gaffer'. It flourished in the service of the Roman Empire and was transplanted to important centres within it. From its original development, probably in Syria, it moved to other parts of the empire, Rome and Cologne in particular. Glass products were made in a number of the major towns and cities of the empire and were spread through trade and colonisation throughout its length and breadth. This created a market for glass products that was to ensure its survival even after the break up of the Roman Empire itself. The model of production was, in Roman terms, large scale, centralised, sophisticated and concentrated within important urban centres. The objects made ranged from batch-produced everyday containers to high quality luxury items made singly or in very small numbers. The strict demarcation between hot and cold (*Vitreari* and *Diatreari*) reflected a simple economic fact. The cutting and polishing of a blown form increased its cost enormously and, therefore, cutting was reserved for high status items. This remained true until the invention of automatic cutting machines in the 20th century. The status, value and rarity of an object when it was originally made does not necessarily reflect its true worth. Values, of course, are relative, but the aesthetic appeal of, say, a Roman square storage jar blown into a uniform mould, to allow for close packing, carries a powerful formal appeal. This is out of proportion to its original value and purpose, and largely because contemporary sensibilities are tuned to the appreciation of a beauty derived from severe, functional limitations.

The Romans overturned many of the basic assumptions about glass they inherited from the Ancient World, none more so than their use of it as a transparent material. This required the development of a consistent decolourising technology to counter the contaminants inherent in the raw materials used to make up glass batch. The technology required to produce colourless glass was sophisticated and therefore only possible within a stable and advanced society. It relied on an empirically (as opposed to scientific) based control of the chemical composition of the basic glass batch. Virtually all natural sources of silica contain contaminants, usually iron, that results in a tinted rather than colourless glass. A major result of the use of glass as a transparent rather than richly coloured opaque material was that it triggered the search for a truly colourless glass capable of rivalling the highly prized rock crystal. Once set in motion this search continued until the development of a 'crystal' glass many centuries later. The Romans began the process by the high value they placed on colourless glass, reserving it for the production of high value items. Nevertheless they did not possess the technology to fully counteract contaminants, and even the clearest Roman glass only manages to limit their effect. The use of decolourisers, usually manganese compounds, was only understood much later and the Romans relied on carefully chosen materials, particularly sand, to minimise contamination. The scientific base for the true control and prediction of glass manufacture remained out of reach until the early 19th century. The hidden areas caused by this lack of knowledge were occasionally glimpsed through accidents of manufacture. The famous Lycurgis cup in the British Museum illustrates this type of occurrence and the value placed on it. It was made from a freak piece of diachronic glass (one that reacts differently to reflected and transmitted light), its uniqueness within surviving Roman glass suggests that it was produced by accident, possibly when a furnace had to be suddenly shut down due to failure. The resulting glass lump with its mysterious shift of colour, from green (reflected) to pink (transmitted) was important enough to be elaborately carved into a cage cup, and later, set into a gold base.

The success of the Roman factory system, set up for maximum efficiency round hot glass furnaces, created a model that dominated glass production to the point where it excluded all other processes. This meant that during its virtual monopoly of hot glass shaping (from the 1st century AD to the early experiments in sheet glass making in the late 17th century) all glass objects had to be made from the basic premise of glass gathered on a blowing iron or scooped up by an iron ladle. In addition to containerware (to which blowing was pre-eminently suited) tiles, window panes and scientific apparatus, to name only a few, also had to be produced. It is, for example, the least efficient method by which to make large, even, flat sheets of glass, and as a result this essential commodity remained small, crude and expensive until the dominance of glassblowing began to be challenged by pioneers like Bernard Perrot in the 1680s.

Glass quality and variety reflected the health of the Roman civilisation and reached a peak at the same time during the 2nd and 3rd centuries AD. At this peak the range of products, production and decoration methods were greater than they would be until Venice at its *apogee* in the late 15th century. This included a wide range of cold and hot processes, among them enamelling. Despite the centralised and anonymous nature of much of the Roman glass industry, it is clear that within this there was still scope for the production of stunningly original work by a single workshop or small group of workshops within the same geographical area. An example of this is the incredible 'snake-thread' decorated ware adorned by the application of delicately twisted threads to their surfaces (see opposite). They are tentatively associated with a glass making centre at Cologne, known to be an important manufacturing focus. They date from the 3rd century and represent a remarkable inventive response to the limitations of hot glass. Despite the fact that it is obvious that the trails were fabricated separately and gently pressed onto the surface of the vessel they are almost impossible to duplicate. The crisp, separate detailing of the threads can be so easily lost during their attachment to the wall of the host form.

The stability brought to the empire in the 4th century AD by Constantine and Christianity enabled glass to continue as a mass produced material. During the century, however, as the central cohesion was gradually lost, glass production centres began increasingly to reflect their regional influences, and, with some exceptions, the more sophisticated techniques became less widespread. The break up of the empire, first into East and West, and later into chaos, meant the end of centralised glass production. Nevertheless, glassmaking was able to survive the end of the unified Roman system and adapt to the needs of a new, fragmented, world order. The

destruction of an essentially urban civilisation and its replacement by a network of local interests had profound repercussions on the way glass was produced, and on the objects made. During the Roman Empire, glassmaking was based in large, well organised factories, served by access to raw materials from across the empire and was part of an economic system based on trade and commerce, when the empire fell, the circumstances of glass production changed. The primary result of this break up was the demise of the more specialised and sophisticated decoration techniques, particularly cutting, polishing and enamelling. Even glassblowing itself became gradually pared down to its essentials. Simple procedures like mould blowing disappeared as glass-making shifted from urban centres to rural locations near fuel sources, and in the process became vernacular in character. The precise way in which the baton of glassmaking was passed from Roman to post-Roman would largely determine the course and nature of its development for the next seven centuries. With the barbarian invasions, glassmaking ceased in the West; fortunately it continued in the Eastern Empire long enough to ensure its survival, and also allowed the incoming armies of Islam to add these remnants to their own glassmaking knowledge and thereby facilitate its next great flowering.

The break up of the Roman Empire caused glassmaking to evolve into two different types, reflecting the two different civilisations contained within it, East and West. The Eastern Empire, dominated as it was by the establishment of the capital of the Christian Roman Empire at Constantinople drew on the influences within its new limits. The new capital was built on the site of the ancient city of Byzantium, and its eastern cultural influences caused glassmaking to develop in a very different way to the other half of the old Roman Empire. From its establishment in AD 330 to AD 1204 when it was sacked during the Crusades, aspects of glassmaking that died out in the West were kept alive. Although not enough glass from the early Byzantine period has survived to recreate its exact development, there remains enough evidence to suggest that certain important ways of working, using and valuing glass flourished. The ability to make clear glass and decorative techniques like

The classic 'snake-thread' vessel, commonly known as 'the masterpiece'. Probably produced in the first half of the 3rd century AD. *It is difficult to accurately describe the technique, as it has not been possible to replicate this effect. It seems likely that the convoluted thread patterns were produced independently from the blown body. They would have been picked up ready formed by pressing the flattened blown form on to the arranged threads. The extreme skill required and the rarity of such items suggests that production was restricted to a small group or even a single workshop.*
Romisch–Germanisches Museum, Cologne.

109

cutting, enamelling and gilding are demonstrated in the few surviving examples. Glass making remained an urban art, patronised by the wealthy, the Church and the royal court. Glass was used for the production of high status items, such as jewellery, mosaics and even chalices for the Christian mass. In the West glass was produced locally, reflecting local needs, raw materials and making systems. The ability to achieve a colourless glass by a careful selection of raw materials became impossible and glass inevitably showed the character of local silica and flux within its body. This contaminated range, of mainly greens and blues, could be modified by the inclusion of a limited number of additives, to produce a palette of earth colours. Glassblowing was still exploited for its ability to produce containers for domestic use, but they now reflected materials like horn, leather and ceramic instead of silver or gold. These shapes, in turn, derived from the practical ergonomic nature of their use, and to the cultural attitudes to eating and, particularly, drinking. Vessels meant for liquid consumption were designed to be held by the rim (cone beakers) or in the palm (palm cups). They did not have stable bases, reflecting the custom of drinking without putting the vessel down until empty (when it was placed upside down on its rim); such a vessel would 'tumble' if put any other way, hence 'tumbler'. The conventional wineglass, with its bowl made stable by an attached stem and base, owes much of its form to this inheritance. These objects, made by the most basic glassmaking methods, relied on a high level of skill on the part of the maker. Despite their apparent limitations the objects made were among the most sophisticated in the history of the material. This refinement derived from the pared down elegance of the cone beakers on the one hand, to the exuberance of the cabbage stalk beakers on the other (see above right). They both relied on an organic relationship between glassmaker, form and material (see opposite). All aspects of the making system were dependent on hot glass working; detail and decoration were achieved primarily through the addition of trails and blobs of semi-liquid glass. The objects that resulted reflected the tribal habits and identities of the communities they served: the Franks in France and Germany and the Anglo-Saxons in Scandinavia and Great Britain. Production was centred in forested

A Frankish claw beaker of the 7th century AD. *The reduction in the range of glass processes after the fall of the Roman Empire led, paradoxically, to an increase in the creative use of basic, hot glass, methods. The development of the 'cabbage-stalk', and its use to elaborately transform the simple cone beaker, is one of the high points of glassmaking.*

Broadfield House Glass Museum. Photo, David Jones.

areas that provided fuel for the furnaces, and plants to burn for potash. The furnace was a simple device built of clay, and constructed round a ceramic pot. A tradition became gradually established whereby glassmaking centres were set up within the forests of northern and central Europe. Glass was made in them for only a part of the year, restricted to the warmer months, housed in semi-permanent structures like logging camps (see p.112). The heat produced by the furnace would be made to serve a

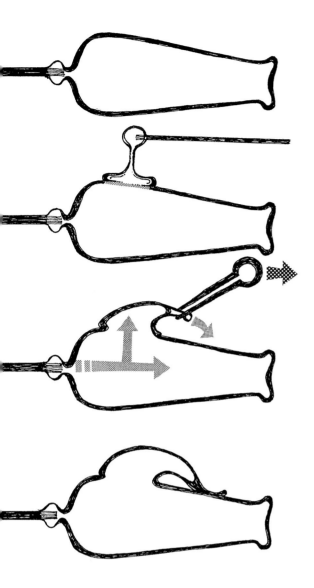

The production of a 'cabbage stalk'. While the main body of the beaker is still attached to the blowing iron a prunt of hot glass is stuck to the wall. This softens the wall at the point of contact and allows this section to be inflated whilst the rest of the form remains rigid. After inflating, the resulting protrusion is pulled with pincers and attached to the exterior surface of the beaker. This procedure is repeated for each stalk. The vessel is completed by the attachment of a punty iron and the shearing, and opening up of the rim area.

number of functions through subsidiary chambers to the main glass melting area. These would utilise the excess heat given off by the founding process to both dry and pre-fire fresh ceramic pots, and to anneal the finished articles. These chambers would usually be built above

the furnace to make best use of the rising heat. The technology was simple, based on a verbal non-written tradition residing in groups of people who often carried the knowledge within families. As G.O. Jones[28] commented in our own era 'Glass technology has grown up largely as an empirical study, separated from the mainstream of physics and chemistry'.

The fact that glassmaking was not based on any precise system of symbolic abstractions but on observation, constant repetition and ritual, and carried as tacit knowledge, aided both its survival and spread during a period when centres of learning were under attack. This mobility was helped by the simplicity of the furnace and the reduction of the process to basic glass manipulative skills. There has never been another way to pass on physical skills other than day to day instruction, a feature that was built into the system early on, and which still operates today. The furnaces and glassmakers were taken to the fuel sources and created a type of production, Forest glass, that was to remain the only remnant of glassmaking in the West from the fall of the Roman Empire until the start of the Renaissance. Such a system was vernacular in essence and empirical by nature. The objects made reflected this in their forms and use, relating to parallel vernacular traditions in furniture, architecture and allied metal, wood and ceramic artefacts, rather than following fashions emanating from the European courts and aristocracy. Nevertheless, the paradox is that such an apparently unsophisticated system did not limit either creativity or the development of objects of great beauty. The limitation imposed by the restriction of decoration to that which could be achieved through the use of small additions of hot glass during the making process, led to an inspired expansion of its decorative and formal potential. The prime example being the simple addition of a blob of hot

Pilchuck glass school, Seattle, USA. The world-famous Summer School was established in a wooded area in the early 1960s. Despite the difference in time, the central structure housing the furnace and blowing shop is remarkably similar to the structures erected by the European glassmakers in forested areas during the Dark Ages.
Pilchuck Glass School. Photo, Russel Johnson.

glass, known as a 'prunt'. Its origin was as a simple aid to handling by the creation of a surface protrusion from an otherwise smooth form. It evolved from serving this ergonomic function through several centuries into a rich decorative effect caused by the functionally unnecessary repetition of the prunt until, in many examples, it dominated the entire shape of the vessel. Even so, the way in which the simple prunt became a defining feature of Waldglas is still remarkable. The fact that an addition of a small amount of hot glass has the effect of softening the area it sticks to was exploited both by pushing in to the interior space of the vessel (thumb beaker) and by expansion to create extrusions (claw beaker). In addition a rudimentary form of pressing was developed, possibly suggested by wax seals, to give surface texture to the hot glass, the so-called 'raspberry prunt'. These became the exuberant signature of

Waldglas at its best and were a triumph of invention in the face of extreme limitation. The contaminated glass, with its green/blue hue or range of simple earth colours, purple, yellow and brown, were given character by random bubbles and streaks and complimented rather than diminished these magnificent objects. The expressive reaction of their anonymous makers to the living, mobile, malleable material on the one hand, and the restrictions imposed by circumstance on the other created the circumstances from which these objects emerged. The nature of glass as a material ensured that their forms and surfaces carried an accessible, frozen record of their time at the furnace.

Vernacular traditions are characterised by their linear continuity, achieving a sophistication of technique and form over time that often rivals the self-conscious stylistic efforts of a single named artist or designer no matter how great. The vernacular glass tradition of forest glass achieved its greatest continuity and refinement in the forests of Northern Europe. Written records are, naturally, uncertain but it seems likely that aural accounts of forest glass being produced in some areas continuously from Roman times to the 19th century are correct. An example is the forest of La Thierache on the borders of France and Belgium. Apart from England (which switched to coal in the 17th century) glass furnaces were fuelled with locally obtained wood well into the 19th century - St Gobain, for example, continued using wood until 1852. The system of glassmaking evolved to the point that it was perfectly suited to, and dependent, on certain types of forest. The forests of Darney in Lorraine were typical, supplying calorific woods in the form of oak and beech, ferns to burn to make flux, local sand, and communication in the form of roads and the river Saone. The universality of wood for fuel meant that forest glass houses often shared areas with other makers like potters and ironfounders. The essential nature of the forest glasshouse was as a small, low-tech operation and it was not amenable to large scale improvement without altering its character; expansion was achieved by an increase in glasshouse numbers. The products, although produced for practical, local use evolved to a point where their sheer quality made them sought after by higher levels of society. The *roemer* of the low countries was a particular example, evolving over the centuries into a drinking vessel of great style and character. Its trailed foot, formed complete over a wooden mandrel, was as much a trademark of Waldglas as the use of the prunt. The appearance of these glasses in the paintings of Dutch masters, and their use for diamond point engraving, proved that the products of the forest glass houses had transcended their practical origins. The northern heirs to

the Roman tradition had come full circle.

The development of glass in the eastern section of the Roman Empire had, by contrast, taken an entirely different direction despite sharing the same origins. As the empire in the West broke down, in the East it divided into an area based on Constantinople and one dominated by the rise of Islam. Muslim power created an empire and civilisation that was eventually comparable to that of the Roman Empire at its height. After its establishment in AD 632 it generated centralised, sophisticated urban order, just as one was being destroyed in the West, and in doing so ensured the survival of types of glassmaking and decoration that would have otherwise disappeared entirely. Without this, not only would the magnificent glass of Islam not have been produced, but the whole subsequent development of glass in the West would have taken a totally different direction. Without its access to Islamic glass technology and skilled makers during the 12th and 13th centuries, Venice would not have been able to develop its own industry. The verbally based, empiric system that sustained glassmaking during Europe's Dark Ages was, in the East, matched by a written academic tradition based in Islamic libraries and Universities. This reflected the survival in the East of high quality sophisticated glassmaking, by its nature dependent on a more scientifically based understanding of the principles underlying its production. This knowledge in the form of written treatises by leading Arab scholars was based on an academic, but pragmatic, approach and ensured that the more complete multi-stage processes developed under the Romans, survived; the use of decolourisers, cutting, carving and enamelling not only continued but were added to. This became incorporated into a growing tradition that evolved in a different direction to its western antecedents. The West has often failed to acknowledge its debt to Islam, but the evidence is there both in the nature of the contacts between Venice and Islam in the crucial century (13th) prior to the flowering of its own glass industry, and in Arabic words such as *alkali* for glass flux. In the East glassblowing continued to be the main forming method, with containerware as the prime output. Typically, Islamic glass followed the shapes of those in ceramic and metal, and through this developed into a range of forms characteristic of Islamic style and decoration as well as adapting to the specific conditions of the Middle East. The tendency for precious liquids to evaporate in the dry heat was countered by the use of long necked containers that were to become such a feature of Islamic glass (see right). Glass compositions were based on scientific principles, and as a result were more predictable, varied, and sophisticated than in the West. The use of manganese dioxide was known to act as a decolouriser to create near-colourless glass, while coloured glass was the result of a wider and better understood range of additives, resulting in a distinct, rich palette of colours. It was, however, to be the development of specialised decorative techniques and procedures that marked Islamic glass. Although the glassmakers and scientists of the East were able to produce clear or coloured translucent glass, their love of surface richness in architecture, ceramic and metalware inspired them to further develop enamelling on glass and to transfer their ability to lustre from ceramic to glass. In enamelling, finely crushed glass is mixed with a soft, flux glass and carried in a medium (oil, honey or gum). This is applied by brush to the surface of a cold, pre-blown vessel. This is then heated until the flux runs and gels the glass enamel permanently to the host surface. Although enamelling was known to the Romans it was the Islamic artists who brought it to maturity in the magnificent mosque lamps of the 14th century AD (see opposite). A close examination of an example of Islamic enamel work reveals its refinement, control and sheer artistry. The linear outlines are painted with a flat, delicate technique, using a specially fine enamel that sits on the surface. The colour infil, on the other hand, is much thicker and is made up of much coarser and denser glass grains, which, when fired, create a strongly hued,

An Islamic water-sprinkler of the 18th century, demonstrating the sheer quality of Islamic glass technology and glassmaking. The sophisticated sinuous shape gives expression to a form initially developed to counter the effects of evaporation in the dry heat of the Middle East.

three-dimensional coloured effect. This is, of course, deliberate and demonstrates a high level of predictive control over the mixing, application and fusing of the enamels. It is extremely difficult to fire enamel on to the surface of a blown vessel without deforming the original vessel. The use of a flux glass (with a low melting temperature) as an addition to

A Mosque lamp of the 14th century. The scale of this object makes it a fine example of glassmaking, whilst the quality of the glass and the use of painted and fired enamels display the mastery of glass technology and techniques at a time when glassmaking in the West had been reduced to its most basic.
Trustees of the Victoria and Albert Museum, London.

115

the enamel causes it to become sticky enough to adhere at a lower temperature than the deformation of the glass of the host vessel, although only by a few degrees. The difficulty in terms of heat control, and its even distribution, becomes increasingly more exaggerated the larger the vessel to be enamelled, and enamelled mosque lamps are among the largest such objects in the history of glass. There are two main methods for heating the vessel to fire the enamel surface (firing in a kiln and rotating in the furnace mouth), and because of precedents set in Islamic ceramic lustre ware I strongly favour their use of a kiln to achieve the necessary conditions. This would indicate that Islamic glassmakers combined a wide range of allied skills and practical expertise. This enabled the design and operation of kilns which maintained an even heat throughout and which could be monitored and controlled accurately to achieve very precise temperatures. The cold, blown vessel was placed in such a kiln with the enamel decoration in place and the kiln was lit and carefully raised in temperature until the enamel fluxes reached softening temperature and bonded the crushed colour on to the glass surface. As I have indicated, this is also the way in which lustre patterns were fired on to glazed ceramic and glass. This is a process in which the salts of a variety of metals (gold, silver and copper), are mixed with oil and painted; the resulting pattern is fired in a kiln and creates a fine, reflective metallic surface burned into the top glass skin. Lustre painting on glass was a particular Islamic achievement and underlines their mastery of theory and practice. Despite the extreme probability of kiln techniques being employed to fire enamel there is another way which has distinct advantages and which at least deserves description. Instead of placing the object in a kiln it is warmed in the lehr and placed on its rim. This allows it to be re-attached to a punty iron and rotated in a glory hole or furnace mouth until the enamel flux softens. This method, although apparently rare, has a number of specific qualities to recommend it.[29] It does away with the need for a separate type of kiln and it enables the fixing of much thicker layers of enamel because the host vessel can be allowed to soften slightly without distortion as it is spun on the iron (see right). Enamelling by this method was noted in Venice in the 18th century and there can

A rare, late 15th-century Venetian wineglass. It is a hybrid, showing a dependence on metal goblets of the same period, and displaying clear crystal in combination with dark coloured glass. The decoration includes the application of gold leaf and crushed glass enamel. Pattern and techniques came through contacts with the sophisticated glass of Islam. The gold leaf and enamels were fixed to the glass by rotating in the furnace mouth, rather than in a separate kiln firing.

Photo, Derek Balmer.

be no doubt that Venice learned its enamelling processes from Islam, in addition to the majority of the glassmaking knowledge it used during its own pre-eminence.

Venice originally developed a glass industry to produce sheets of richly coloured glass for mosaic tesserae. These sheets were small, gathered and poured using a ladle and resembled slabs of toffee ready to be cut into small squares. Simple poured discs were also made in a wide range of colours, opaque and transparent, and traded throughout the world as raw material for enamellers to crush into powder. This industry was well established by the 9th century and provided a strong root on which additional expertise obtained by trade and treaty with the East could be grafted. Venice as a City State grew in importance during the 11th to 13th centuries by exploiting its unique position in the Mediterranean. It became an important centre for learning and the arts, in which glass, true to its nature, flourished. The power wielded by its fleet allowed it to further exploit its advantageous trading position on the Adriatic, achieving a virtual dominance of trade with the East. Its links were strengthened by an important treaty, signed in 1277, between the Doge of Venice and the Prince of Antioch to facilitate the transfer of technology between the two centres. Through this, the conditions were established that allowed many secrets of glassmaking to be brought to Venice at a crucial point in its development as a world power. Everything necessary was imported directly from Syria, raw materials as well as physical expertise in the form of Syrian/Arab craftsmen. This helped to create the cocktail of conditions that led to the flowering of glass in 14th to 16th century Venice, which, in addition to the production of some of the finest glass ever produced, dominated glass for centuries. The main ingredients of this cocktail were:

1 An existing Venetian industry,
2 An influx of knowledge, skill and materials from Islam,
3 The increasing European importance of Venice in terms of trade, commerce and culture,
4 The wider cultural context of the Italian Renaissance in Painting, Architecture and the applied arts and, not least,
5 The quality of raw materials available to Venetian glassmakers.

By the 15th century Venice had emerged as one of the five most powerful states in Italy. Its unique position on the Dalmatian coast meant that by 1500 its republic was a major political power in Europe. Nevertheless, it was the fortuitous contribution of a local raw material that added the important final ingredient and allowed the development of *crystallo*.

It had long been known that the cleaner and whiter the silica that was selected to form the basis of the glass batch, the clearer (and more like the prized rock crystal) the resulting glass. The Venetian glassmakers used flint pebbles from local sources to crush into the silica that provided 70% of the typical glass batch. Even in our own era high quality glass is referred to as 'Flint' glass. This, together with the soda derived from the burnt ash of the local maritime barilla plant, created an unusually clear, hard glass which also had an extremely long working time. This is the time between its removal from the furnace or a blowing iron and the point when it becomes too rigid to continue shaping without re-heating it. In addition it was strong and extremely malleable. This combination made it a unique glass for the 15th century and formed the basis on which all other aspects of Venetian glass depended. This combination of clarity, malleability and long working time created a material that perfectly matched the complex formal language of the High Renaissance (see overleaf), even though these qualities were largely outside the control of the glassmakers themselves. However, this is perhaps too retrospective a judgement: a more accurate assessment might be to celebrate the creative reaction of the Venetian craftsmen to the gift of this unique material, for both were needed to ensure the full flowering of the 15th and 16th centuries. The crystal glass, as it rapidly became known, seemed so well suited to the stylistic context of Renaissance Venice only because of the inventiveness of the makers. There was certainly nothing inevitable about it despite the inherent qualities of the glass itself.

Despite its reputation as an equivalent of natural rock crystal the Venetian crystal glass was, in practice, not particularly clear or light refractive. Only by blowing it extremely thinly could it be described as clear or colourless. Any build up of glass within an item made from it, for instance in the stem of a wine glass, created a dark mass of glass that did not hold or focus light, certainly not in comparison with later lead crystal or potash rich crystal of the 17th and 18th centuries. The fact that their glass became renowned as crystal was, as much as anything, a tribute to the ways in which Venetian glassmakers devised shapes and techniques that emphasised its transparency while disguising its lack

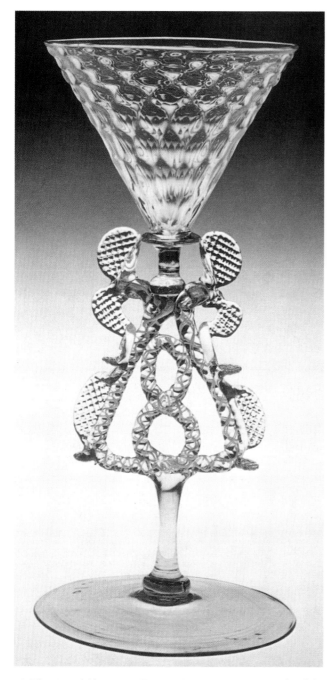

A Venetian 16th-century Dragon Stem. A prime example of the exploitation of the malleability and ductility of liquid glass in the creation of form and decoration. A skilled glassmaker would have made this object in about 20 minutes. Compare this to the production of the same forms in metal.

Photo, Derek Balmer.

hollow. Much skill went into achieving this level of control. An ideal Venetian wineglass was thin and transparent to the point of invisibility in direct contrast with its equivalent in later lead crystal.

Venetian glass of the 15th century is hybrid by nature, absorbing influences from Islamic originals, particularly in terms of decoration, and contemporary Renaissance silver. The results were vigorous, powerful, but perhaps a little uncomfortable, particularly in contrast with the later maturity of 16th century crystal. The Islamic style of gilding and enamelling sat a little uneasily on forms borrowed from silver originals, the glass itself was often coloured and/or opaque. These rich colours formed a backdrop to the sophisticated enamel and applied gold leaf decoration adapted to create the commemorative goblets that characterised this period. The physical qualities of the gilding and enamel work, its density of colour, and three dimensional feel, suggests that it was fired on by spinning the re-heated goblet in the mouth of the furnace rather than by firing in a kiln. The flared lip of the goblet could also be formed at the same time as it would have certainly become soft enough to be reshaped. Gold was applied, not as a liquid lustre but in the form of small patches of gold leaf, cut and stuck to the cold surface of the glass with an organic binder that would burn off when re-heated. It would become permanently fused to the surface of the glass during the spinning and re-heating procedure of enamelling. Continuous lines were formed painstakingly by overlapping sections of gold leaf, creating a characteristic seamed effect that can be clearly seen on close examination. The effect is generally richer, and carries a textured quality missing from the flat uniformity of lustre.

In the 16th century such decoration became much less important, following the lead of painting and architecture, where the surface richness of the quattrocento gave way to the high Renaissance and its accent on form rather than detail. The qualities of *crystallo* had been developed to a point where it could be exploited for its inherent quality as a material. Its malleability, strength and working characteristics enabled the glassmakers to give full reign to their extrovert natures, often echoing the elaborate *contraposto* of Renaissance painters in the convolutions of twisted glass. Also during this period glassmakers themselves grew in importance and prestige, resulting

of refractive qualities. It is no accident that their glass was not cut or facetted, for, at its best, Venetian crystal was blown extremely thinly, any build up of glass was avoided, stems, for example, were blown

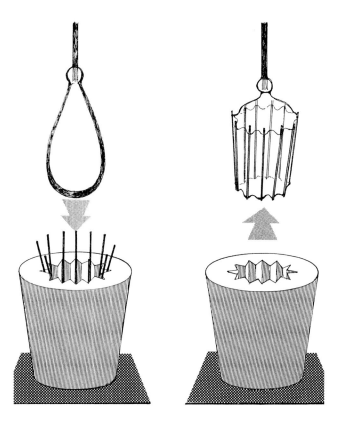

The principle behind the Venetian blown forms heavily decorated with embedded canes, depends on picking up the canes on the initial gather prior to final shaping. Just as there are different end results, e.g. latticino and vitro da trina, there are different ways of organising this. Here, a regular star-shaped dip-mould is used, into which glass canes have been placed. When a gather is blown into the mould it picks up the canes in a regular pattern. This can be repeated using different pattern dip-moulds to achieve a crosshatched pattern of rods. The rods themselves were often twisted and/or multi-coloured. Once the rods were in place the glass was re-heated and made into the desired item.

Latticino *goblet of the late 16th century, showing the masterly use of complex twisted canes to make up the body of the vessel. These were arranged within a ridged dip-mould that supported them vertically, and were picked up on the surface of a bubble blown into the mould. This could be repeated to build up layers of rods and special effects such as air pockets between rods.*

Photo, Derek Balmer.

in greater artistic, expressive freedom. The objects they produced occupied a high position within the stylistic hierarchy of the society they served. They bore the same relation to the high arts of painting, sculpture and architecture as did the English crystal of

the 18th century, both deriving from, and making a contribution to, high points of their respective cultures. The parts played by the nature of the two versions of crystal within these different cultures was considerable. The long established tradition of glass making in Venice, possibly stretching back to Roman times, also made a major contribution to the development of Venetian Renaissance glass. The production of coloured glass for mosaic and enamel work was adapted to provide coloured canes that were used in conjunction with *crystallo* to produce a wide repertoire of effects. These were based on the application of canes to the body of blown objects during their manufacture (see left and above). The various ways in which these were applied, attached, combined and distorted during blowing and hot forming were creatively exploited to yield a wide range of effects, many of which became synonymous with Venice. Terms like 'latticcino' or 'vitro de trina' have been coined to describe the effect imparted to the glass, and the techniques associated with them have become part of glassmaking tradition.

The development of true Venetian crystal seems to have been virtually complete by the second half of the 15th century when two named glassmakers were given sole rights to produce the 'new crystal', although Angelo Barovier, of the famous glass dynasty, was also involved. By 1550 it was the standard by which all quality glass was judged and the island of Murano contained thirty-six glasshouses (compared with two thirds of that number today) and it is estimated that three thousand people were employed in glassmaking, although this included bead making, cane, and enamellers glass cakes, in addition to vessels.[30] Venice became the first major exporter of glass since Roman times. In true glass fashion, Venetian glass reached its peak at the same time as Venice itself, but its dominance of quality glass production in western Europe ensured its survival beyond the inevitable decline of Venice. Not only was its glass sought after but many attempts were made to produce it outside Venice, not least because of the large amounts of European money that flowed into Venice to purchase it. The quality and style of the products restored to Europe the concept of glass as part of a cultural hierarchy of materials, taking its shapes from fashion rather than from within a vernacular tradition. The glassmakers themselves enjoyed an equivalent rise in status, although only to the *populare* or third grade, below the nobility and citizens, who were forbidden to practise mechanical trades. Much has been made of the edicts that attempted to prevent glassmakers leaving Venice with their precious skill and knowledge, and their existence underlines the fact that glassmaking expertise resided in people rather than books. Although written accounts had emerged since the end of the Dark Ages they were written by academic clerics like Theophilus (12th century) who was not a practitioner and claimed that he 'learned by looking and listening', not doing. As a result, his book, *Diversarum Artium*, was like most accounts until

Neri in the 17th century, written from the viewpoint of an observer rather than a practitioner. It is hardly surprising therefore that Venetian glassmakers could command large sums and advantageous working monopolies in European countries that yearned to produce their own *façon de Venise*. However, they needed more than just glassmakers, they also needed to develop a glass, preferably from locally available materials that was capable of rivalling *crystallo* itself. The search for a glass that was good enough to break the dominance of Venice began in earnest in the early 17th century, and as usual with glass the journey was to end up nowhere near its original goal.

Until the industrial revolution in the 19th century glass was made by mixing natural materials, i.e. silica and plant derivatives. Furnaces were constructed from stone and pots were made from fired, local clay. A typical mix would comprise silica 60%–70% by weight (this could be in the form of sand or, in the case of Venice, crushed flint pebbles from the river Ticino), ash 15%–20% (obtained by burning plants with a potash content) an admix of lime for stability and trace elements to confer brilliance or to counter the effects of contaminants. These were known as decolourisers or 'glassmakers soap'. The improvement of trading conditions allowed glassmakers to once again import quality ingredients in their quest for quality. For the first time since the break up of the Roman Empire barilla was imported into Europe from Alicante to provide an alternative to ferns or bracken. It is no accident that many of Europe's major glasshouses (many still in operation) were founded as part of the spread of *façon de Venise*: Hall in the Tyrol in 1534, Innsbruck in 1563, Munich in 1584, Leerdam in 1560, London in 1571.

The dominance exercised by the example and ideal of Venetian crystal continued well into the 17th century. A number of centres were so successful that it is virtually impossible to differentiate between *façon de Venise* products and the real thing. Germany, Austria, Silesia, Bohemia all sought to improve the quality of their rich potash glass, and by absorbing Venetian stylistic characteristics, raised the status of their repertoire of vernacular forms, which included the use of enamelling, itself derived from Venice. 'A crucial ingredient of glass development during the

17th century was the patronage of Princes and Kings to certain gifted individuals'.[31] This encouragement and protection from harsh economics occurred in France, and especially in Germany, where Friedrich Wilhelm of Brandenberg (1620–88) built a glass house in 1674 to support his hobby. He encouraged the development of quality glass, particularly the perfection of a crystal glass. In 1678 he engaged J.F. Kunckel to direct the experiments and by the end of the century high quality glass was being produced in parts of Germany which, although it was different in character to Venetian glass, deserved the epithet 'crystal'. Much of this search had changed its approach during the 17th century due to the publication in 1612 of a treatise on glassmaking by an Italian, Antonio Neri (see right). As Polak puts it, 'Neri's book was sensational because it dealt only with glass (unlike Theophilus), and because it was written to instruct'. This was because Neri was essentially a hands-on practitioner. His book was devoted to glass recipes which he claimed were 'all tried out and done by myself.' It was reprinted three times during the 17th century and translated by Dr Merret in 1662 in London with extensive commentary and additions. Importantly Merret was a scientist and scholar who added an extra dimension to the book, particularly concerning English conditions. This version was itself translated and added to by Johann Kunckel in 1678 as *Ars Vitrearia Experimentalis*. His contribution was, like Neri's and Merret's, based on a sound mix of practical experiment and scientific knowledge. Some of his work can be traced to an important Arabic text of the 9th century, thereby establishing the probable link with Persian glass and its influence on the West. The importance of these texts is in the way it added a scientific dimension to the hands-on mysteries surrounding glassmaking. In doing this it created the circumstances that were to lead to the development of a glass industry that, by the 19th century, was served by a glass technology that enabled both control, and an expansion of glass products and production systems. The search for a high quality glass that was capable of replacing Venetian crystal also led ultimately to the end of the monopoly of glass manufacture by glasshouse methods. Even during the golden age of Venetian

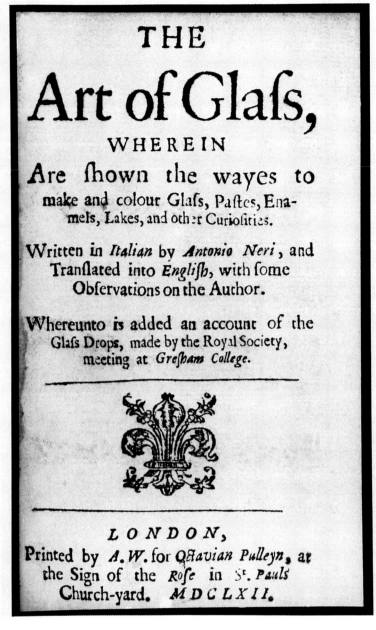

The front page of the English edition of Antonio Neri's book The Art of Glass *of 1662. Note the reference to the 'glass drops', being the famous Prince Rupert's drops. In placing the mixing and founding of glass as a material on a firm, practical base, he laid the foundations of the science of glass technology.*

Science Museum Picture Library, London.

glass during the 16th century, the prime method of shaping glass was through hot manipulation centred on glassblowing. These techniques were organised into a factory system on the island of Murano and followed a production model established by the Romans fifteen centuries previously. Even new techniques like latticino were essentially elaboration's of the same age-old hot glass procedures. Such was the domination of this system that all glass objects needed by society were produced within these factories, and were governed by the limitations of its central skills and procedures. The range of products was understandably, wide, and included containerware of all kinds from simple bottles to elaborate goblets, scientific apparatus, apothecaries jars, lamps, lenses and flat glass for windows and mirrors. Not all of these products could be adapted easily to the available methodology of the blowing shop. Possibly the case of mirror glass production was the most extreme, and its solution started the break up of the dominance of the single process multi-product factory. Although its development pre-dates the true industrial revolution by almost a century, its story provides a model for all of the single product systems that came later.

Mirror glass, as opposed to window glass which could be produced efficiently by the glassblowing, cylinder and crown methods, had to be made thick enough to allow for polishing and grinding to create a distortion-free surface. It was produced by gathering, or ladling as much glass as possible and pouring it on to a flat, metal surface, while attempting to smooth and flatten it. The sheet of glass obtained was small and irregular and had to be painstakingly ground and polished before a reflecting metal foil was fixed to one surface. This had the effect of making mirrors prohibitively expensive. They became sought after, high style constructions of many smaller pieces of costly mirrored glass. The cost of large mirrors during the 17th and 18th centuries was so high their production and use was limited to important public buildings and the houses of the wealthy. As the demand grew, a powerful economic force was created that fuelled the creative imaginations of a number of entrepreneurs. The high cost of mirror glass for his architectural projects caused Louis XIV to set up a factory devoted solely to the manufacture of sheet glass for mirrors (it is now St Gobain). In doing so he broke the traditional link between the process and the need for a diversity of products. Instead, he isolated a single product and encouraged a complete re-think of production methods. This enquiry broke the mould of traditional working systems and became the forerunner of many similar endeavours to achieve a new way of producing any single product, in this case large sheets of glass. In this arrangement a period of experiment and refinement has to be allowed for, including the investment of a great deal of risk capital. This accounts for the way in which such ventures were often undertaken under the patronage of wealthy, high placed individuals. The isolation of a single product allowed the enquiry to start from an entirely different engineering premise to the manipulation of glass on the end of a blowing iron. The French factory was not the only centre for such experimental developments, similar work was carried out in England (this too would develop into a giant of glass manufacture, Pilkingtons).

As usual with such breakthroughs, much depended on the genius of a single individual, in this case Bernard Perrot who set up his workshop in Orléans in 1662, and with the patronage of Louis XIV was able to develop new ways of casting sheet glass. Such was his success that the *Academie des Sciences* awarded him sole rights of production in recognition of his achievement. The desire for mirror glass ensured his success, and its use in the *Salle des Glaces* at Versailles in 1684 created a fashion for large mirrors. The factory of St Gobain was founded in 1693 as a specialist flat glass producer and continues in that role today. Although by 1700

Venice was still the world's largest producer of glass its dominance had been permanently undermined by the forces set in motion by such ventures. Even the product range of the single, central glass house was split during the century so that by the middle of the 18th century three distinct kinds of production had developed based on quality of glass and type of product:

1 Coarse green glass for bottles, made from ordinary sand, unpurified ash and cullet,
2 Purer glass from selected and imported ingredients for middle range domestic ware, and
3 Top quality glass from selected sand and specially refined ingredients, particularly ashes purified by filtering, drying and grinding.

The amounts of glass produced increased to keep pace with demand; furnace design and refractory expertise developed to allow the production of pots capable of melting two hundredweight of glass. To cope with such increases annealing chambers were developed as separate entities capable of holding eight hundred bottles. By the end of the 17th century glass served a wide range of functions that were spread across the entire social spectrum. This was the first time this had happened since the Roman Empire and coincided with the rise of the West economically, culturally and scientifically. The increase in wealth and population created the circumstances for the development of trade, and improvements in product quality and manufacturing methods. Despite the emergence of larger efficient factories that produced increasingly specialised products in large numbers, the dominance of glass-blowing still had a hundred years to run. It was not until the late 19th century that the erosion begun by individuals like Bernard Perrot was completed, as its products were adapted by mass production methods one by one.

The legacy of Venice meant that by the start of the 18th century most European countries had been forced to establish their own indigenous glass industry. This was driven by a number of imperatives, not least the huge costs of imports from Venice to satisfy the increasing demand for quality glassware. The main requirement was a glass of sufficient clarity, and lack of contaminating colour,

capable of consistent production at the manufacturing source. At first the new centres, in England, France and Holland especially, concentrated on the production of *façon de Venise*, but the success of the search for a crystal glass in England were to lead to both a new material and a new style.

The development of English lead crystal (see overleaf) at the end of the 17th century appears, with hindsight, to have been created by the coming together of a number of different factors, which resulted in an almost inevitable outcome. However, the facts point to a number of important creative individuals who in reality manipulated the components to cause their advantageous synthesis. As with other European countries, Venetian craftsmen were encouraged to come to England by lucrative contracts which allowed them monopolies of the production of Venetian style glass. These met with limited success in terms of both quality of product and material, and extant examples of such objects are rare. However, the high cost of imported Venetian glass ensured the continuation of such ventures, but it was the contribution of a chain of unconnected events that were to lead eventually to a true English crystal, and to the development of a world-class glass industry. This chain was set in motion by the needs of the British Navy, which required vast quantities of wood for shipbuilding. The glasshouses in southern England especially (established by French Huguenot refugees) were burning wood at such a rate that a law of 1615 made it illegal to use wood for glass furnaces. This caused the first shift of fuel for glassmaking in its long history and led ultimately to the use of coal, and the inevitable migration of glass industries to areas of Britain with surface coal and good communications (Stourbridge and Newcastle). Nevertheless, coal had many drawbacks as a fuel for glassmaking. It was unsuited to the open pot furnaces with their oxygen rich atmosphere that had evolved for use with wood. A simple substitution of coal for wood meant that black tarry deposits constantly fell into the glass mixture and contaminated it. To counteract this the English developed a special closed pot with an opening in its side to provide access to the glass. Coal also needed higher temperatures for efficient combustion and the English developed the brick cone that surrounded the furnace and created

A group of late 17th-century lead crystal vessels. The development of full lead crystal seems to have had the advantage of being the right material, in the right place and time. Having said that, there was nothing inevitable about the way in which 18th-century glassmakers created a distinctive style that exploited the particular qualities of the material. The two central items show evidence of criselling. A characteristic of this early group is its use of forms from Venetian and Waldglas originals. These do not marry particularly well with the nature of lead crystal, especially in comparison with the more austere, architectural forms that characterised its use in the 18th century.
Trustees of the Victoria and Albert Museum, London. Photo, Daniel McGrath.

an updraft. The cone was a uniquely English feature and was once a common feature of the industrial landscape in glassmaking towns like Stourbridge in the Midlands. The shift from wood to coal, and the adaptations to the process this necessitated, also created the circumstances by which oxide of lead could be added to the glass batch. The open pot with its oxygen rich conditions would have oxidised the lead to create a heavily contaminated glass. The search for a workable version of crystal-like glass in

England was not, initially, a success. Various inducements and monopolies were granted to various entrepreneurs during the 17th century to encourage its development. That so many people were prepared to risk money and invest their efforts in such a venture was an indication of the potential profits that would follow success. It was not until the experiments of George Ravenscroft, where he added red lead oxide to the batch mixture that all of the circumstances came together, both accidental and deliberate, to create a unique glass in England in the closing years of the 17th century. Despite early setbacks caused by 'criselling' (unstable mixtures creating a glass that eventually decomposed) the new glass was a great success. The rare, and valuable, examples of Ravenscroft glass show the quality of the new material and the extent to which it differed from the Venetian version it had originally sought to imitate. In fact, apart from its colour, what Ravenscroft had discovered was, in most respects, the complete opposite of its model: lead crystal, as it rapidly came to be called, was refractive, dense, soft, and its particular qualities became more intense as it was built into solid forms like wine stems. It had a very short working time, and could not easily be re-heated to soften it for re-working as this led to the lead oxidising as a grey film on its surface. It was thick and could not be easily manipulated and was therefore totally unsuited to the exuberant excesses of Venetian style glassware. This was rapidly realised by the English glassmakers, and it is here that the last important influence made itself felt, that of stylistic context. Lead crystal was developed at the end of the 17th century and was fully established as the premier glass of choice by the first decade of the 18th. It was therefore ready to contribute to the flowering of the arts that characterised England during this century. During this period England was to enjoy prosperity, a growing importance in world terms and develop an equivalent artistic presence, particularly in architecture and the applied arts. The new glass with its unique properties was worked within a rich and burgeoning formal and stylistic context, capable of representing it to the full. Social behaviour developed too, with dining, entertainment and etiquette making ever more complex demands in terms of specialised serving, drinking and containerware. Within the formal restraint of English neo-classicism the restrictions of lead crystal were an asset rather than a limitation. Just as Venetian crystal had been well suited to the curvilinear excesses of High Renaissance style, so too English crystal was the perfect medium for shapes derived from Palladio and Adam (see right). The architectural baluster was particularly well chosen to provide the model for stemware. Where the Venetian ideal of a hollow stem was the creation of a gossamer thin support for an equally thin bowl, the English baluster was solid, and

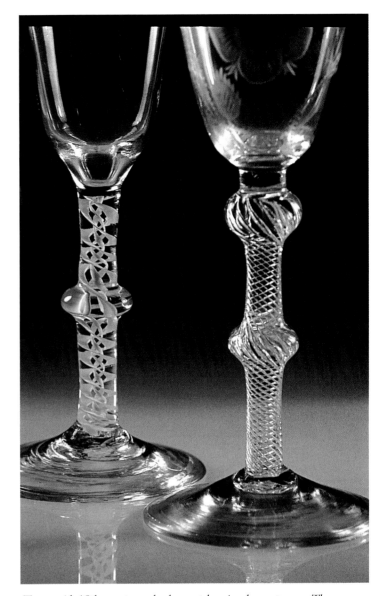

Two mid-18th century lead crystal wineglass stems. The development of stems containing twists of air or enamel, although the inventor remains anonymous, was a major creative exploitation of the material. The physical process of introducing bubbles into the hot glass by pricking it and then elongating and twisting to make the stem must have been developed by a glassmaker. The enamel twist was created by the introduction of a small piece of coloured cane and twisting while pulling out the stem. A similar technique is used in the production of marbles, where pieces are cut off and rolled into spheres. The distorting knops are another original design feature associated with lead crystal.
Broadfield House Glass Museum. Photo, David Jones.

in its variation of contour, exploited the luminous, light-refracting material that was its greatest feature. It is amazing how quickly the new material was exploited for its own sake rather than as an imitation of *crystallo*. A range of entirely new shapes were

125

developed that, in partnership with the material, created classic versions of drinking vessels that have never been surpassed, and which have created the bench mark for all new designs. Nothing illustrates the difference between Italian and English glass as much as the way in which English glassmakers elaborated on its light-amplifying qualities by the inclusion of bubbles and glass canes, particularly in stemware. At first bubbles were introduced singly, and the variations in the glass that encased them were used to distort them. Later bubbles were introduced in twos and threes and elongated and twisted as the stem was drawn out, creating the air twist. Canes of coloured glass were also trapped in stems as a variant of this procedure. Although the development of glass design in the 18th century remains anonymous in character, developments like the baluster, air and cane twists are inventions of great genius (see right). Although the general context is provided by English neo-classicism the nature of these developments could only have come from the glassmakers themselves. Where drawings by designers exist, and they are extremely rare, they provide shapes with no indication of how these were to be made. Only the glass craftsmen possessed the hands-on knowledge required to conceive and perfect their procedures. Although we will never know the identity of the individuals who originally created them, they have made a major, lasting contribution to the history and repertoire of glassmaking. Such additions to the vocabulary of glass were essential to match the increasing demands for glass objects, particularly those associated with wining and dining. A new range of words had to be coined or borrowed to describe the proliferation of forms: trumpet, bucket, bell, baluster, knop, etc. So successful was the new industry, built from small beginnings at the end of the 17th century, that by 1745 the government felt able to tax the glass industry by weight of glass produced. Some production moved to Ireland to avoid the tax but the overwhelming majority of factories stayed in England. Of course, not all of them were devoted to the production of lead crystal; during the 18th century three distinct types of glass production and product had evolved. These were:

1 Bottle manufacture, using dark, contaminated glass and concentrating on the provision of large amounts of glass for its glassmaking teams to

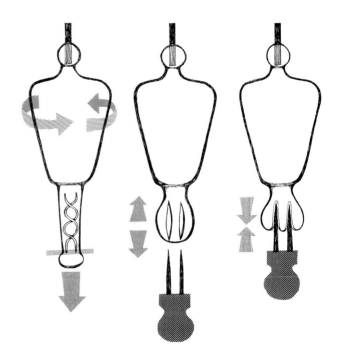

The production of an air-twist stem. The principle is the introduction of indentations into the semi-molten glass, with spikes set into a wooden handle. These become bubbles within the glass when the spikes are removed. As the stem is pulled to shape it, the main body is twisted on the blow pipe to create the spiral, as the bubbles twist around each other. The technique can only have been developed by someone who actually formed glass on a day-to-day basis. The name of its highly inventive originator is unknown.

rapidly convert into large numbers of near identical containers.

2 Flat glass manufacture, using contaminated glass blown thinly by the cylinder and crown methods to provide reasonably clear, if small, sheets of glass for buildings. These two methods provided the bulk of window glass needs until well into the 19th century.

3 Containerware. This covered a range of objects and quality with some factories concentrating on the lower end of the market and only those that catered for the upper strata of society employing true lead crystal. The point at which an object moved from use in one stratum of society's hierarchy to another determined both its shape and the quality of glass it was made from. A prime example of upward mobility being the evolution and elevation of the simple wine bottle from a storage vessel below stairs, to a pouring vessel fit to join the dining room company. The decanter, made from lead crystal and styled to fit its new

surroundings, took over this same function as the 18th century unfolded.

The development of so called Bristol blue and white opal glass were also the results of stylistic influences. Both glasses provided an excellent background for decoration by lustre and enamel, influenced by, and adapted from porcelain.

As the 18th century progressed, the shapes of glassware reflected the general stylistic context in their move toward lightness of form and thickness. While this has sometimes been attributed to the 1745 tax on weight of total production, the influence of fashion was, in my opinion, the decisive one. The dynastic links with the House of Hanover helped to bring to England the cutting lathe that had been adapted from gem cutting in Austria, and which allowed lead crystal to display another of its prime qualities. It was soft, easy to cut and polish, and, of course, highly refractive once facetted. Also, just as with the forms it originally borrowed from architecture, the geometric patterns of neo-classical decoration systems provided the source for cut decoration. This ensured the harmonious, restrained relationship between form and cut decoration that is one of its hallmarks.

Anglo-Irish glass and its production systems became as dominant in world terms as that of Venice had been. This domination continued through the Regency into the early Victorian period with significant shifts of style, but with lead crystal continuing as the prime material, and with production systems remaining little changed.

Although the development of English lead crystal (up to 30% of its volume being red lead oxide) created a glass that set a standard of excellence, the search for a high quality clear glass also bore fruit in other European countries. The long standing glass industries in most major European countries, although based on forest glass production systems, adapted to the challenge of Venice. This originally took the form of a greater control over selection and preparation of the batch ingredients. By the end of the 16th century, for example, Bohemian glass, although still using local materials, had improved purification methods and developed more efficient furnaces. This created a clear potash rich glass that could be formed thick

enough to cut. Carl Lehmann was the holder of the title of 'Imperial Gem Engraver to the Austrian Court', and in 1608 added the title of 'Glass Engraver'. It was the popularity of engraving during the 17th century that drove the improvements in glass batch and glass quality. Engraving a glass raised its price and status and new forms (the pokal, that particular style of engraved, lidded goblet developed in Germany from the late 17th century (see p.40)) were developed to reflect this move away from shapes that originated in practical use. Underlying this was a tradition of gem and hardstone engraving that provided both the aesthetic motivation and the technology that could be adapted to glass. During the 17th century, the use of rock crystal provided a standard of material quality and a format for the transfer of deep engraving to blown glass. Towards the end of the century improvements in glass composition were achieved, through a more scientific approach and a greater knowledge of the roles played by each batch constituent. The addition of chalk to the batch in the 1660s improved the clarity and softness of the potash/silica/lime glass. It was the influence of Kunckel that was decisive, however, with his combination of scientific knowledge and practical experiments. His book *Ars Vitrearia Experimentalis*, published in 1679, built on the work of Neri and Merrett and subjected glass-making to genuine scientific research for the first time. One result of this was the first consistent production of ruby red glass by the addition of precipitate of gold.

Although by the early part of the 18th century glassmaking had evolved into three distinct branches of production, bottle houses, flat glass, table glass (itself divided into flint and ordinary) all of these, despite their differences, were based on the same basic system. This was totally dependent on a consistent high level of manual skill. Skill was a commodity that could only be generated by instruction and constant practice. A glassmaking team comprised a number of specialists and varied from as few as three to as many as seven. The head of the team was the gaffer who was the most skilful and whose skill was concentrated where it was most needed. The other members of the team (gatherer, servitor, marverer, finisher, and taker-in) each performed an important but less skilled role. The importance of skill was recognised and its constant regeneration was built into the system. Despite the fact that time taken from making reduced profits, twelve hours a week was set aside for the training of apprentices, who were given an additional six hours for practice. It took five years to become a gaffer, and to achieve this status required the making of a masterpiece. It is hardly surprising that glassmakers were sought after and guarded their skills jealously. The reliance on natural, local materials and natural manual skills to produce glass and glass products created limits for an industry that, by the end of the 18th century, was expanding dramatically. The demands of a rapidly growing population and the wide range of glass products needed created the circumstances under which the search for easier alternatives to natural materials and skills became worthwhile, and to some extent essential. For example, by 1775 prices of potash and Spanish barilla had risen so much that the French Academy offered a prize of 12,000 francs for a process that could manufacture an alternative. The result was the invention of the Leblanc process that succeeded in making Soda from salt. This was the first step in a mechanisation and standardisation of batch materials. In the 19th century silica for glassmaking became scientifically controlled, prior to this the variation in quality and sources had been extraordinary, from sand, sandstone, basalt, granite, feldspar, obsidian. Ingredients were manufactured from their chemical constituents rather than selected plants or mineral sources like shells. To some extent this mirrored the way in which the skill-centred system was broken apart and re-assembled as mechanisation, with machines rational-ising and largely replacing physical skills. Although this move was led by the need for numbers and economy, the impact on the nature of the end product was equally

dramatic. The way in which glass can be altered through its composition and its unique nature as a material created circumstances in which its transition from hand to machine could be directed by a select band of creative and far sighted individuals.

To set up an enterprise that searched for a new way to manufacture a single glass product rather than to merely improve the conventional way of making it required the coincidence of a number of factors. Such a venture required a large capital investment, luck, talented individuals and time to experiment and perfect processes until they became consistent and repeatable. The element of risk was great, and while such an undertaking is a mainstay of contemporary commercial practice, it was rare in Europe before the 18th century. What made people take such risks was the growing, lucrative market for specialist glass products. It was the very success of the mirror market that exposed the limitations of the traditional glasshouse – its inability to provide larger and more perfect mirrors to satisfy the increasing demand. Three types of item reached the point by the 18th century where such enterprises were worth undertaking. These were bottles, mirrors and optical quality glass. The solution to the individual problems associated with each made a collective contribution to the advance of glassmaking that in turn paved the way for the revolution of the 19th century.

The population of England rose from five and a half million in 1700 to nine million in 1800. This huge increase is one factor in the growth of bottle production. Even in 1700 there were 39 bottle factories producing three million bottles per year. The growth in, and variety of types of drink also made a major contribution to the demand. New processes (soda water), new and better closures (cork), and commercial production (Joseph Schweppe established in 1794) made it both worthwhile and necessary to separate bottle making and to increase production through specific improvements to furnaces and methods. The expansion and refinement of specialist bottle manufactories meant that by 1833 there were 126 bottle factories in England and 240 by 1874.

The larger production system needed was made possible by the new furnace technology brought in originally to burn coal instead of wood. The fact that coal required a revised burning system, raised on a metal grill with a deep ash pit beneath, meant that larger amounts of glass could be founded at one time in the higher temperatures reached. Coal required a higher temperature than wood and was burnt on a metal grill with a deep ash pit beneath (see p.97). The furnace and pots had to be built of stronger, more durable materials to survive both the higher temperature and the corrosive effect of the larger volume of liquid glass. Despite the contaminant effect of burning coal, open pots were used, the new closed pot was developed only for lead glass. The dark colours of bottle glass were not easily discoloured by sulphur deposits and the glass was of a standard soda base. The brick cone (see p.98) was developed by English glassmakers in the late 17th century to create an updraft and increase the oxygen throughout the furnace. This was a specific result of the use of coal and was listed in the French Encyclopaedia as the '*Verrerie Angloise*'. Wood remained the sole fuel for continental glasshouses until well into the 19th century. Despite these improvements bottle making was still exclusively a province of traditional hand forming. Instead of a piecemeal improvement and rationalisation of manually based processes from a starting point of blow-pipe centred skills, what was required was an approach from a different direction.

The demand for, and high cost of,

mirror glass prompted the experiments of Bernard Perrot and yielded the first new glass process for 1500 years. The principle behind the new process was pouring rather then gathering, and it dominated flat glass production until alternatives were developed nearly two centuries later. The procedure involved pouring liquid glass on to a large metal table from a moveable ceramic container called a 'cuvette' although this was replaced by the lifting of the pots themselves. This dramatic shift of attitude to the way glass was manipulated required an imaginative leap that is hard to appreciate today (see overleaf and p.131). The numerous improvements in sheet glass manufacture that followed during the 19th and 20th centuries made the process even more efficient and sophisticated but none were as creatively important as the first. The French factories rapidly exploited their position and by the 1770s were annually exporting between £60–£100,000 worth of plate glass to England. The low cost of coal and the value of the end product led to the foundation of an English flat glass industry based on the French model. Ravenhead was founded in 1773 and began the Merseyside domination of flat glass production. It is hard to comprehend the immense cost of a large sheet of mirror even when made by the radical new methods. In 1756 a sheet of mirror glass 180cm x 120cm (60in. x 43in.) cost £100 retail, an astronomic figure for the time.[32] Given this it is understandable that a British Parliamentary Committee in 1776 recommended the setting up of a British Cast Plate Company 'for fabricating largeglass plates, such as are imported from France, and valued at four to five hundred pounds each.' The capital required was £50,000 and the casting hall built at St Helens was the largest industrial building in the country to date. The process was controlled by a French man from St Gobain. By 1801 the British Cast Plate

(ABOVE) *An example of a Bullseye hand-rolled sheet of glass, showing the unique, organic surface possible by manual methods.*

(OPPOSITE PAGE)
There is still a place for handmade sheet glass in our own era despite the dominance of production by mechanisation. This flexible system, operated by Bullseye Glass Company, Oregon, has two great advantages: it can vary production easily, and is capable of making glass sheets which have a variety of surface textures and patterns. Like similar, individual quality products (such as handmade paper) they are used by artists, designers and craft practitioners.

All photos Bullseye Glass Co. Portland, Oregon, USA.

Company was producing an average of twenty large plates per day, in excess of seven thousand a year. Each plate of course had to be ground and polished by hand to impart the necessary flat surface and high polish required for the mirroring procedure. Although the polishing and grinding stage was rationalised and greatly speeded up during the 19th and early 20th centuries it remained a slow and labour intensive business until it was superseded by the invention of the float process in the 1960s. There is a distinction to be drawn between the invention of new processes, based on new approaches, the development and improvement of existing processes, and the insertion of a new stage or stages to existing processes. Inventions are radical and often revolutionary in their impact. Glassblowing, sheet pouring and pressing are examples. Improvements like the development of the glassmakers chair increase the range of existing ways of working and new stages, like the addition of the roller to plate glass casting, increase efficiency and the quality of the end product.

The third component of the improvement and specialisation of glass production during the 18th century was the search for optical quality glass. The use of lenses for spectacles, telescopes, microscopes, burning glasses grew enormously during the century but was totally dependent on the clarity of the available glass from which these were cut, ground and polished. Glass that appeared bright and flawless in a wine-glass revealed serious optical imperfections (bubbles, seed and striations) when ground into a lens. Improvements in glass technology and production were needed to provide specially clear glass for these purposes. A pot of liquid glass was founded, the furnace shut down and, when cold the glass was broken into hundreds of irregular pieces which were sorted into various sizes to be individually ground into lenses (see overleaf). This was basically the same procedure that had produced the glass blank from which the Sargon vase was cast and carved in 700 BC. Although, by the 18th century, the control and understanding of batch constituents made it possible to eliminate many of the major flaws in optical glass the glass produced was still far from satisfactory. The rewards for the developer of an improved process were large enough to encourage investment and experiment. The breakthrough came when a Swiss, Pierre Guinand, spent thirty years experimenting and, using lateral thinking, transferred his knowledge of metal founding to the production of glass. The metal founded for bell casting had to be of the highest quality and was stirred during production to ensure consistency. Stirring the molten glass proved to have a similar, improving effect on quality, particularly with respect to the elimination of

A pot of optical glass being broken up to yield a large and varied array of irregular pieces. These would have been individually shaped, ground and polished to provide single items. The pot of glass would have been stirred continuously while liquid, to ensure optical clarity. It seems astonishing that this was the only source of such glass until direct casting and pressing became feasible. The two world wars of the 20th century boosted research into the efficient production of optical glass for military purposes.

Pilkington Bros Ltd Archive.

striations in the glass. Although improved many times, this simple concept remains in the production of optical quality glass.

Taken together, the specialised production of bottle, sheet and optical products provided the basis for the full industrialisation of the material during the 19th and 20th centuries. The improvements in furnace design and materials, the experience of founding large amounts of glass, advances in glass chemistry all set the scene for the larger mechanisation to come. This was initially hampered by a number of factors:

1 The success of methods based on empirically derived tradition, e.g., glass had been coloured blue for thousands of years by these methods but it was not until 1733 that cobalt was identified as the source.

2 The fact that, to some extent, glass had been organised into units of maximum efficiency as early as the 1st century AD and it was not until its dependence on hand driven craft skills was challenged by the flat glass factories that the way lay clear for a total shift of approach.

3 The peculiar nature of the material itself. Its viscous semi-liquid state and unique characteristics presented a challenge that was hard to meet from mainline material experience. During the Industrial Revolution a number of crucial breakthroughs were essential if glass were to become part of the overall conversion to mechanised production.

CHAPTER FIVE

The Modern Era: 1830 to the Present

'Glass was considered such a difficult material to handle in the molten state that mechanisation
was introduced later than in most industries.'
L. Angus-Butterworth, *History of Technology*, Vol. IV.

'The art of making glass is entirely chemical.'
Samuel Parkes, 1826.

While the Industrial Revolution was a predominantly Western European phenomenon, it was in America that the first major new glass process to emerge since the invention of blowing developed, at least in terms of containerware production. A look at the background circumstances reveal why this happened.

THE DEVELOPMENT OF PRESS-MOULDING

I have tried to put forward in this book the argument that glass production reflects the general health of its host society, and that it only thrives and develops within technically sophisticated cultures. True to its cuckoo nature it needs a wide range of other material technologies to draw support from in order to exist at all. The history of glass in the United States appears to bear this out, at least until the 19th century. There were numerous attempts to transplant glassmaking on to American soil during the early colonisation period of the 17th and 18th centuries. Those ventures that did succeed were very much in the European mould, Stiegel and Amelung for example. The fact that they succeeded where many others failed was in the main due to the way

in which they adapted sophisticated European practices to the limitations of American conditions. The problems encountered were common to all systems of manufacture in the New World, not enough skilled labour, a scarcity of parts and materials and a growing demand for goods from a burgeoning population. The best of American makers circumvented the limitations by the power of invention. They were able to look at old problems through new eyes, and come up with alternative methods that were suited to the circumstances and needs of the new republic. (In this, of course, they mirrored a similar political process that had led to the new constitution.) Lack of craftsmen and women and sophisticated traditions was met by the invention of revolutionary machines that altered the landscape and society, from combine harvesters to nail-making machines.

The invention of the glass press was part of this general, inventive movement and, in its own way, was as radical as any of the other inventions made during this period (see p.136). The invention, (as opposed to improvement or development) scrambled the stable, traditional glassmaking equation. Almost at a stroke it shifted the balance of power from the skill of the glassblower to the designer and maker of the metal mould in which the molten glass was given

Detail of a pressed dish from a dressing table set from Eastern Europe, 1930s. Despite the low cost of pressed items, quite sophisticated qualities were achieved through skilful use of material and process. Here the imagery has been pressed into the surface of the glass, leaving it as a concave depression. This has been acid etched and the flat surface of the glass ground and polished to heighten the contrast.

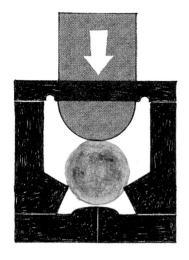
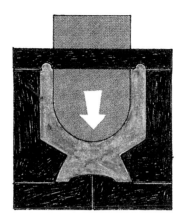
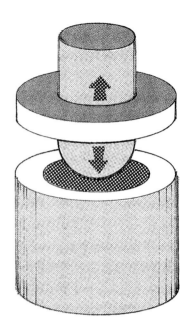

The three parts of a pressmould:

a *The body, split to allow removal of the glass object.*

b *The plunger that 'presses' the glass into the mould and at the same time forms the inside of the glass.*

c *The cap ring. This sits on top of the mould and is perforated to allow the plunger to pass through it. It forms the rim of the glass and allows the depth of the plunger movement to vary slightly to allow for different quantities of glass.*

form. While glass had been pressed before in its history, by hot glass being pushed into simple clay or metal moulds, the first American patent [33] defined a totally different process, one based crucially, round a repeatable system. The theory behind it was relatively simple, and as usual relied on the way in which glass creates a skin at its surface as it cools from liquid to solid. Compressing a given amount of glass between two metal sections, one convex and one concave, gave form and texture to inside and outside surfaces at the same moment, and enabled hollowware to be formed without glassblowing skills. The basic system in a crude but workable form was in use by 1830 and its success ensured its rapid improvement. The development of the cap ring made the process more sophisticated by allowing the mould to adapt to the slight variations in the amount of glass placed in it for pressing. This was the only aspect still governed by human skill and it was impossible for a skilled gatherer to dispense precisely the same quantity of glass for each press. The system in its simplest form was operated from a basic, hand driven, side lever press, borrowed from the metal working industry, and required only a single movement of the lever to bring the top and bottom moulds together to create an object. This simple but highly inventive procedure revolutionised glass container production, and provided a new view of glass as a material capable of being produced by mechanised, non craft methods. The break with traditional craft skills also ushered in a perception of glass design, where form was determined totally by the person(s) who designed the production system (see opposite). Such a system had to work within the limitations of hot glass and the way it reacted to the metal surfaces of the mould. As with all hot glass forming it relied on the way in which glass cools by first creating a skin at its surface.

MASS PRODUCTION

To a large extent the invention of the press, and its subsequent development into a complex multi-part system capable of great variation, democratised glass, turning it into a wide range of cheap, readily available commodities for domestic use and decoration. The growing population of America and Europe provided a ready market for such goods; but pressed glass was

136

(ABOVE) *The automated production of television screens by pressing at Schott Glass, Germany. The precise amount of hot glass is automatically measured and sheared. It drops down a chute and is delivered into the mould at exactly the correct temperature.*

(BELOW) *The glass is pressed by a shaped plunger into the mould. The automated production system and the need for a quality end product means that every aspect of the glass, temperature and timing have to be orchestrated within very strict limits.*

Both photos Schott Glass, Germany.

clearly inferior to the blown and cut glass it sought to replace, particularly in terms of its surface. Lead glass, with its short working time is extremely difficult to press and therefore soda lime glass had to be used. In addition, early pressed glass suffered badly from surface distortion caused by an inability to control the temperature relationships between the glass and the mould. When glass is pressed by metal formers the skin created can be chilled if the temperature differential is too great, so instead of an even surface the glass is marred by riffles caused by surface movement. This undesirable texture was eventually eliminated by improvements in glass composition and mould temperature monitoring and control, for although the mould has to be hot it also has to operate at a lower temperature than the glass to prevent it sticking. Before such control was developed, the designers reacted creatively to this problem and simply disguised the defect by covering the surface of the mould with low relief pattern drawn, not from other glass processes, but from Victorian decorative art in general. The result was the famous 'Lacy' glass which, despite its obvious drawbacks and crudity was a brilliant solution to a problem, and one which owed nothing to traditional forms of glass decoration or manufacture. The pressing process allowed a semi-skilled glassworker whose job was to estimate and gather the correct amount of glass needed to fill the mould, and a second worker whose part was to shear the liquid glass into the mould and operate the mould mechanism and glass press lever, to produce five times as many products as a skilled blowing team with up to six members. The shear mark, where the skin of the glass was cut to release it from the iron, and the mould seams were often obvious across the object produced, particularly with complex shapes whose moulds were multi-sectioned and hinged. These shortcomings were disguised by turning the hot mass of glass as it fell into the mould so that the scar fell across the base of the object (see overleaf), and by improvements in mould technology and by slightly re-heating the pressed object to fire-polish the surface and remove slight imperfections. In addition, acid polishing or acid etching were used to improve and vary the surfaces, and add apparent sophistication to the machine made product.

This view of a Sowerby's pressed item displays the shear mark where the liquid glass was cut to deliver the correct amount of glass. The resulting scar was hidden where possible on the base (or interior) of the object. The multi-coloured glass is another example of the confidence of the large manufacturers and their search for novel colours and effects.
Broadfield House Glass Museum Photo, David Jones.

EUROPE

Pressed glass was a runaway commercial success, and expanded rapidly in America and Europe, particularly Britain where the Sunderland firm of Sowerby's boasted of operating the largest pressed glass factory in the world by 1880. It employed over five hundred people and produced thirty tons of pressed glass items per week. Pressing was still carried out by hand-operated side lever machines despite numerous improvements to aspects of the process (see opposite, top).

Given the fact that pressing was a process that existed to make glass products cheaply and in vast quantities it is astonishing how much variety and individuality the designers demonstrated. A single mould was an expensive piece of high quality engineering and had to operate continuously at high temperatures. The only way in which this outlay could be justified was for each mould to produce thousands or even millions of objects during its working life. While this is a simple fact of mechanisation it is also usual to design bland objects which enjoy a long and wide popularity, and which are capable of surviving sudden shifts of style. Yet what characterises pressed glass between 1830 and 1920 is a constant, daring, inventive variety of shape, pattern

and texture. Bizarre novelty shapes, requiring the development and production of multi-sectioned moulds contributed to production catalogues containing thousands of items (see opposite, below). Factories like Sowerby's had to maintain and store all of their moulds, although there is some evidence that some moulds were shared between manufacturers, and made the trip across the Atlantic to and from America.

NOVELTY

It is equally surprising that the designers exploited the full range of pressings formal vocabulary, apparently uninhibited by the history of glass. While it is true that much pressed glass of necessity imitated cut and blown glass, what is really impressive is the volume that did not, preferring instead to plunder the broader history of decoration and form in all materials and cultures for shapes, patterns and textures used within eclectic mixed patterns (see p.140). Pressing was certainly 'the most technologically advanced, and economically significant glassmaking technique introduced since the invention of blowing'[34] but it was only one of the inventions that were to accompany and follow it in the next century. Reyner Banham has described a

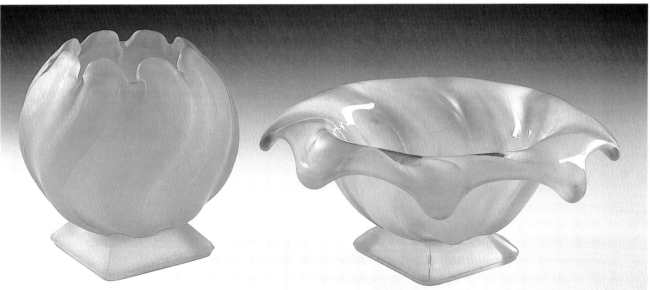

(TOP) *A group of pressed iridesced tiles by Tiffany. He brought together three aspects of the material and its history to produce these superb Art Nouveau architectural features. His research into glass compositions (via skilled technologists) resulted in the varied colours and effects that characterised his 'favrile' blown glass. This was combined with simple hand pressing, and the use of metallic salts in solution sprayed onto the hot glass to create the light refracting surfaces. He was inspired to develop a chemical equivalent by the iridesced surfaces of ancient glass created by burial in acid soil.*

Hawarth Art Gallery, Accrington and author's collection.

(ABOVE) *Two pressed glass dishes by Bagley, Nottingley, South Yorkshire 1930s. Both objects were pressed in the same mould, originally with straight, vertical sides. Picked up by the foot in a gadget, the sides were re-heated to ensure their flexibility, and distorted by either folding out or folding in the vertical section. Despite the downmarket image of much mass-produced pressware, great ingenuity was often brought to bear on their design and manufacture, as in this example where radically different forms were produced from one mould.*

A group of pressed items made by Edward Moore and Company, Tyne Flint Glassworks, South Shields, 1886 and 1887. This group demonstrates the level to which simple pressing evolved by the late 19th century. Although cheap to produce and buy, and imitative of blown and cut glass, these items are sophisticated in terms of their use of the process. Pressing fully three-dimensional forms with feet and handles required complex mould technology, and the quality and clarity of the glass shows a sophisticated control of glass founding and temperature.

modern product as an object that is the result of the identification of a single need, and a production system capable of its manufacture in large quantities (see p.135).

SINGLE-PRODUCT SYSTEMS

During the second half of the 19th century the three aspects of glassmaking that had been semi–mechanical were bottle making, flat glass manufacture and pressing. However, crucial parts or aspects of the established procedures were difficult to rationalise and created limitations that acted as a brake to full mechanisation.

NEW FUELS AND MELTING SYSTEMS

Some of these came from the need to use outdated fuel sources and technology and a continued dependence on manual power sources. St Gobain, despite its lead in flat glass manufacture was still using wood for fuel in 1829. This placed strict limits on the size and effectiveness of furnaces, as did the use of copper casting tables with their tendency to warp and split. No alternative was available until cast iron plates could be cast large enough by the early 19th century. Improved fuel use and new sources were crucial to the further development of manufacture on a large scale. Although coal was a more effective heat source than wood it needed the understanding of combustion contributed by the iron smelting industry, and the resulting improved furnaces. The attempt by Bessemer to apply his steel making expertise to glass production in 1846 used a continuous melting system rather than crucibles, and although it was not successful initially, it established ideas and principles that were eventually to become the norm. The use of gas as a fuel made it possible to exercise greater control over furnace temperature and, therefore, to adjust the viscosity of the glass very

Sheet rolling. By the late 19th century the production of rolled sheet for window glass had developed to the point where casting furnaces poured their contents out under rollers that pressed it into continuous sheets of flat or patterned glass, depending on the roller used.
Pilkington Bros Ltd Archive.

quickly to that required by machinery. It also helped America to become, by the early 20th century, the container capital of the world. The natural gas fields in Ohio caused the bottle making plants to develop close to this new cheap and abundant fuel.

The development of steam and, later, electric power allowed the industry to break free of the limitations of manpower alone, particularly in respect of scale and speed of production. Despite this, new, efficient and trouble free systems required the co-ordination of all of these new elements, and it frequently took many years of experiment to perfect a new complete system. By contrast, well established, if hybrid, methods were at the peak of their development, and resisted replacement for a long time. When, in 1850, Chance Brothers of West Bromwich[35] were given the contract to produce 8 million square feet (about 1 million square metres) of sheet glass for the Crystal Palace building for the 1851 exhibition in only eight months, they produced it by the cylinder method. The project involved the production of 200 tons of glass above their normal output and required the importation of thirty extra workers from France. The firm supplied a total of 300,000 individual panes

of flattened (but not polished) cylinder glass 49in. x 10in. (125cm x 25cm).

ROLLING-MACHINES

While aspects of traditional glassblowing systems remained within new manufacturing methods, the craft itself only managed to survive as a coherent totality by recognising and exploiting its craft qualities and ethos. During the 19th century existing products were re-stated in terms of mechanised production, and new glass objects were brought into being as single, isolated mass products. Systems that had already made the break with age old systems, like flat glass for mirrors continued their onward development. The early casting system was supplemented by the use of massive cast iron rollers that squeezed a continuous ribbon of flat sheet glass hundreds of feet long in a single operation. They were finished by steam-powered grinding and polishing. New motive power sources allowed the use of power and weight that would have been impossible by manual, craft means. Once again the possibilities inherent in the new technology were quickly and creatively exploited (see previous page). Rollers could be polished for producing clear sheet or complex surface pattern could be pressed into the glass by the use of patterned rollers; the pattern being quickly changed by replacing the roller. The enormous variety of patterned glass sheet owed nothing whatsoever to traditional glass processes, and derived from a recognition of the possibilities of the new system and the dense, printed, embossed and woven patterns of the Victorian or Art Deco interior (see right).

AUTOMATIC PRODUCTION

There was invariably a point at which traditional methods could no longer compete with the new mass production systems. A case in point was the incandescent light bulb which was originally produced by blowing, until the growing demand meant that it was worth the effort and investment required to develop a machine capable of meeting the demand. Containers of all kinds were subjected to the same treatment: bottles and jars for the new consumer products, and drinks, preserves, sauces and cosmetics all sought to have their brand identity established and recognised by the distinctive nature of their patented containers, the most famous being the *Coca-Cola* bottle first produced in 1884. The economic pressures and potential rewards were so great that the development, through continuous improvement, of fully automatic bottle and jar machines became inevitable. There remained, however, a massive drawback to this development, the nature of the material of glass. The machines that were designed used rationalised versions of the age-old hand and mouth movements of the glass blower. Each aspect of the blowing process, particularly the gather, pre-shape and inflation stages had to be mimicked by the machine. Fortunately, compressed air technology made the inflation stages possible, otherwise the process could not have been perfected. These separate forming stages, each one of which had to be developed as a procedure, were combined with the power and speed of the machine to produce vast quantities of near identical objects with the minimum of human

"CIRRUS Pattern"—one eighth full size.

"CREVASSE Pattern"—one quarter full size.

Two rollered patterns from the 1920s. A change of pattern meant the removal of one roller and its substitution with a new one. The rollers were expensive, highly engineered items, a fact that led to the gradual reduction in available patterned glass sheet from the 1940s.
Pilkington Bros Ltd Archive.

intervention. The fully fledged automatic bottle machines of Michael Owens in the early years of the 20th century were preceded by numbers of systems and devices that solved part of the problem but which could never add up to a fully automatic system. They were, however, part of a forward momentum which ensured the eventual solution of the hardest parts of the problem. Without doubt the greatest obstacle was the first step in the process, the delivery of a gob of molten glass of the right size, shape and viscosity to the machine. Here, the attempts to rationalise the craft methods failed and a

Pressed vase by Lalique from 1929. A brilliant example of design for a specific process. The artistry of Lalique exploited the vocabulary available through the technology of pressmoulding. The quality of the glass, and the flawless control over the process resulted in the production of a classic design, totally suited to its material and process.

Broadfield House Glass Museum. Photo, David Jones.

totally new approach was required. As a result most machines still needed the attentions of a skilled gatherer to feed the machines until the 20th century. The genius of an individual like Michael Owens was required to achieve the breakthrough: he used suction to gather and shape the glass to feed his 1903 machine. Even this problem broke into several others and the final perfection of the complete process took many more years of work. His first A type machine had an output capacity of 125 gross in 24 hours and its labour costs were one

tenth of the semi-automatics.[36]

THE PROBLEM OF THE INITIAL GATHER

The achievement of the delivery of a pre-shaped gob of molten glass to the mould required the development of press and blow technology to shape the molten glass (although the viscosity was higher than for hand means) before it went into the mould. This ensured an even distribution of glass and a partial shaping, compatible with the final form. These systems by the first decades of the 20th century allowed the production of vast numbers of sophisticated forms. A combination of press and blow actions accurately delivered gobs of molten glass to metal moulds at lightning speed, where compressed air inflated them. The *Coca-Cola* bottle with its distinctive shape and impressed name could be made in a few seconds. In the hands of a designer of genius, René Lalique, the automatic press and the press and blow machines could be made to form works of great quality and character (see left).

SPECIALIST PRODUCTS

Other machines were developed to produce an increasing range of products (see overleaf, left hand column, and p.145, top picture), tubing, fibre, rods, lenses, the list is, literally, never ending. All of these separate products were given their own individual machinery plant and patents. Where the circumstances that supported mass production did not exist, i.e. large numbers of identical objects, traditional craft methods were, and are still relevant. The production and testing of prototypes, or the need for a specialised object are examples. It is surprising how many of these are to be found in military and scientific fields, particularly where a new idea is being tested. The combination of methods of glassforming that are thousands of years old and the production of groundbreaking, experimental work is a strange but effective one.

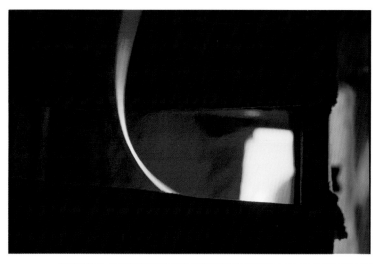

Grinding the fresnel lens segments. This was a precision operation, with the angles calibrated by systems that held and presented the glass to the rotating grinding wheel. The operator is applying carborundum to the wheel with a brush.

Pilkington Bros Ltd Archive.

(TOP AND ABOVE) *The production of glass tubing made using the Danner process. The diameter and wall thickness can be determined precisely by the speed at which the tubing is pulled from the mass. The complexity of the machine controls this speed, and directs the movement of the tubing. It is a contrast between organic glass and mechanisation.*

(TOP) Schott Glass, Germany.

(ABOVE) British Glass Manufacturers' Federation.

LIGHT-HOUSE LENSES

For many years Chance Brothers of West Bromwich England produced the bulk of the world's lighthouse lenses. Many of the smaller ones were of a standard form and could therefore be pressed, but the larger, constructed, multi part lenses were like the lighthouses themselves individually specified (see above, bottom picture on the oppsite page, and pp. 146 and 147). To

(OPPOSITE PAGE)

(TOP) *Lengths of tubing being finished by flame polishing the cut ends. Much of this tubing is produced as an intermediate form of glass, and provides the small-scale container industry with a partly formed glass from which to make phials for medication.*

Schott Glass, Germany.

(BOTTOM) *Casting glass for lighthouse prisms, 1930. Two gatherers pour glass from gathering irons into a simple mould of iron, while a third follows them around and flattens the glass. Although this system seems initially to be an extremely crude one to serve such a precise function, two factors should be borne in mind: the quality of the glass, made under strict conditions, and constantly stirred to ensure optical perfection; and the precision grinding and polishing that give final shape and surface to the glass. The completed metal and glass constructions were calibrated to send light precisely across miles of sea.*

Pilkington Bros Ltd Archive.

A metal armature. In order to present the greatest possible amount of glass, metal constructions of great refinement were developed by Chance Brothers. Each installation was of individual design and construction, and took many months to complete.
Pilkington Bros Ltd Archive.

make them Chance Brothers used a system that employed a hybrid of hand skills and mechanised certainties. The sections were cast oversize by hand into fairly crude moulds, and polished on a specially built machine that ensured their precise dimensions and their accurate function and assembly. Other

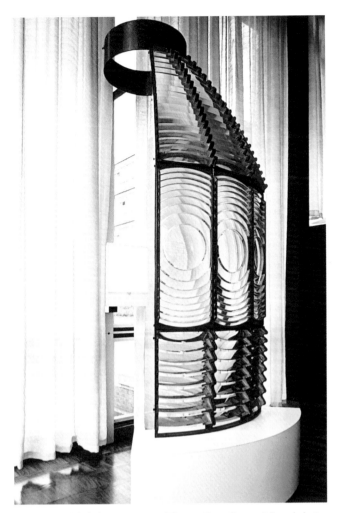

A completed lighthouse section. The quality of material and design caused even government officials to remark on the severe beauty of such objects. Despite their practical purpose, they remain for me some of the most impressive glass artefacts ever produced.

Pilkington Bros Ltd Archive.

notable examples include the Mt Palomar reflector [37] and other large glass blanks, where the kiln itself is a one off and becomes the mould for the single item.

THE FUTURE

The sheer adaptability of glass as a material has ensured its survival for five thousand years. The fact that it is a supercooled liquid, and as such is a loose solution rather than a fixed, stable compound has meant that it can be varied easily, and the definition of glass can be set within wide limits. This has allowed, for instance, the substitution of potash for soda or the addition of lead without the end result losing its unique glassy signature and identity. Its properties can be changed by such variations, and through the current level of scientific understanding and control, glasses can and are designed to fulfil very specific purposes. It has also enabled the development of such material hybrids as glass/ceramics with their heat resisting properties based on an almost non-existent expansion coefficient. The space shuttle is covered in a protective layer of such tiles and yet they are cut and fitted individually in very much the same way as the mosaics at Ravenna or the stained glass at Chartres.

The fact that the properties and behavioural characteristics of glass can be designed to vary so widely means that it can be made to display properties that do not coincide with normal perceptions. In certain uses it can be stronger than, and preferable to, steel (for resisting atmospheric pressure). At other times it can be used for its extreme flexibility (glass fibre). Neither of these uses has anything to do with transparency or any other traditionally held view of glass. The material is used across the widest spectrum of human activity: science, art, design, architecture and engineering. It has been an essential part of human endeavour for at least five thousand years and yet is vital to the space programme. In the service of each aspect of progress it has used one small part of its multiple, myriad personalities. The fact that Corning glass recently stated that seventy percent of its current products had not been in production ten years previously illustrates both the flexibility of the material and indicates its likely long term survival. The new glass compositions that are brought into being at the rate of fifty a day also suggest that in its survival for the next five thousand years it will continue to reveal new versions of itself for use by humankind.

CHAPTER SIX

Glass as a Design Material since 1850

'Design organises the efforts of other arts and crafts, giving
order and purpose to production.'

The transformation of manually driven craft systems of production, from the only way to produce goods, to a small, specialised tributary of mainstream industrial production, created two revolutions. The first, as described, was the growth of specific, single product systems based on a cocktail of forces. New technology, new power sources and burgeoning market forces led to a bewildering array of new inventions in terms of machine processes. The second, caused by the establishment of an industrial order that swept craft-based methods to one side, was the redefinition of the crafts themselves.

THE SURVIVAL OF CRAFT METHODS

Although these methods shrank to small remnants in terms of total production they did not die out completely and the story of their survival is another illustration of the depth and flexibility of the craft approach in general, and that of glass in particular. The fact that the range of historical glass processes in use today is greater than at any time in its history, is explained by its transformation from a material to a medium.

When the traditional glass factories of the 19th century gradually lost their monopoly of glass production, they were increasingly left with the residue of their product ranges that could either not be easily mechanised or could not justify the investment required. This was mainly comprised of decorative art glass and high quality, traditional domestic ware (particularly stemware). Not only were these difficult to mechanise, even partially, but an important part of these objects' status and value lay in the fact that they were handmade. Gustav Weiss pointed out the difficulties that surrounded any attempt to mechanise the traditional goblet form, 'Their complicated form necessitated several machines working together, one group blowing the bowl, stem and foot, and others pressing, putting the parts together.' The survivors from this period continue today, producing and marketing handmade items with a heavy emphasis on their quality, and its foundations in traditional virtues. The continued survival of handmade, decorative items and their partial evolution into domestic art glass was the result of a slightly different equation of forces. Domestic items that were bought and valued for their decorative and stylistic qualities remained well suited to production by craft methods, within small factories. The demands of fashion for novelty and constant evolution of style were met by the ability of these factories to vary production without a large shift in tooling and machinery. It was also fortunate that this change occurred in the second half of the 19th century for it coincided with an enormous appetite for extravagant colour, form and texture. Wages for even highly skilled glassmakers were relatively low [38] and time could therefore be expended on hand decoration to achieve the necessary stream of constantly changing designs.

Convulvulus vase, Stevens and Williams, 1884. A classic example of all of the trends in late Victorian glass rolled into one. A tour de force on at least three levels: (1) Material – the precise novel colours produced by a full understanding of the chemistry and technology of glass, and deliberately intended to be eye catching in a highly competitive market. (2) Form – rich, inventive, convoluted, eclectic and skilful. (3) Making – requiring not only dexterity but also the development of new tools to form details such as the individual flowers. These devices and the design of the items were the work of John Northwood, a man who epitomised the energy and invention of the late Victorian period.
Broadfield House Glass Museum. Photo, David Jones.

THE TRADITIONAL FACTORY SYSTEM

During the 1870s and 80s the surviving factories maintained an enormous range of items, the pattern book of Thomas Webb in Stourbridge contained twenty-five thousand items during the period 1840-1900. The inspiration for the complex, eclectic designs was drawn from a wide variety of sources, many of which had only recently become available (see previous page). Owen Jones Grammar of Ornament and the public displays of wide ranging historical artefacts in the new museums were typical sources of both technical and formal elements. The type of items produced were often not intended to be very practical and could, therefore, have bizarre combinations of decorative features that would rule out any function beyond that of mere display. This was particularly true of the English factories, who produced uninhibited exuberant objects that contributed to the expression of high-Victorian style. Most such factories possessed their own engineering workshops which could rapidly and cheaply produce moulds, tools, devices (see right), and gadgets very quickly to achieve a particular effect specified by the designers. The split between designer and maker became pronounced, and as a result many glass objects became, for the first time, associated with the names of the people who brought them into being (see opposite), after thousands of years of anonymity. The history of 19th and 20th century glass is very much bound up with the careers of well known designers: Carder, Northwood, Gallé, Tiffany, Dresser, Lalique, and later Aalto, Toikka, Sarpaneva, Vallien and Sottsass, to name but a few. Despite their differences many of them shared the fact that they did not actually form the glass themselves but relied instead on prototypes or prescriptions (drawings, profiles) to communicate their ideas to the mould-maker or craftsman. This represented a split from the more integrated and organic systems, and its establishment as a model of practice for craft based industries had a profound effect, both on the industries themselves and on the emerging designer/maker ethos in the crafts.

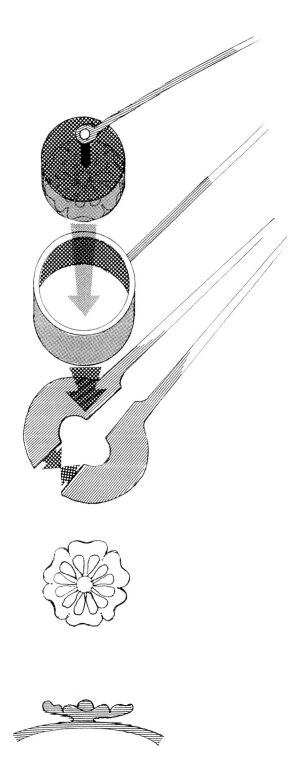

A diagram of one of John Northwood's patented tools. This was a hand-held pressing device which allowed the glassmaker to press a three-dimensional flowerhead from a simple application of hot glass. The function of such tools was not so much speed as novelty, as the quality of the flower added a unique aspect to the items they decorated. The tool comprised three sections all connected to the same stem. The split ring held the bulk of the glass blob away from the wall of the vessel, and the die with the flower engraved on it formed the flower when pushed into the central section which contained the lateral flow of the glass.

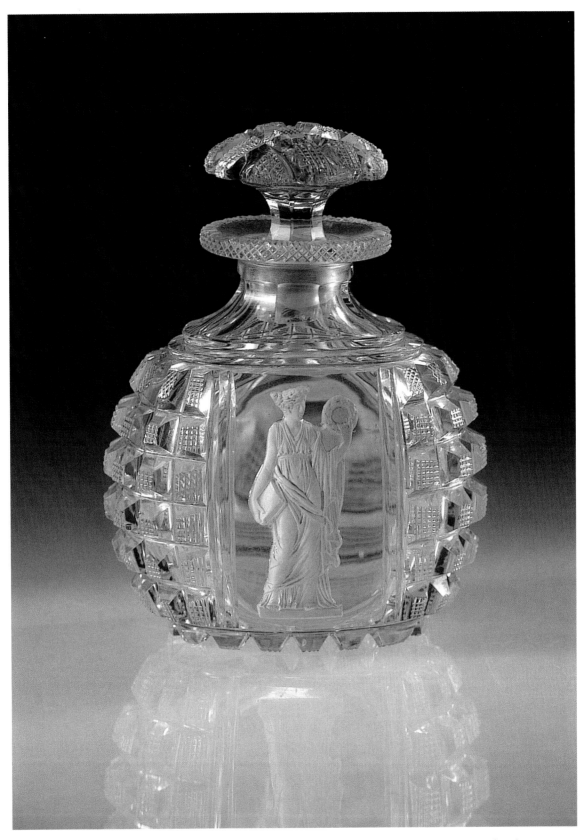

A 'sulphide' by the great Victorian glass entrepreneur Apsley Pellatt. An example of the inventiveness of 19th-century glass designers in their search for new effects to market. The technology and process required to make and encapsulate a cast medallion into the wall of a clear glass vessel took skill and perseverance. From the 1820s.
Broadfield House Glass Museum. Photo, David Jones.

Two 'flower' vases produced by Richardson's in 1900. The development of purely decorative glass forms without even a residual functional element led to the production of items such as these individual flowers. Handmade, they used glass that changed colour when heated, and relied on a range of making skills including shearing, trailing and pincering. These traditional manual skills were allied to the new science of glass technology in the form of heat sensitive 'striking' glass.
Broadfield House Glass Museum. Photo, David Jones.

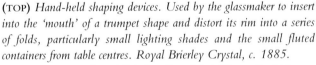

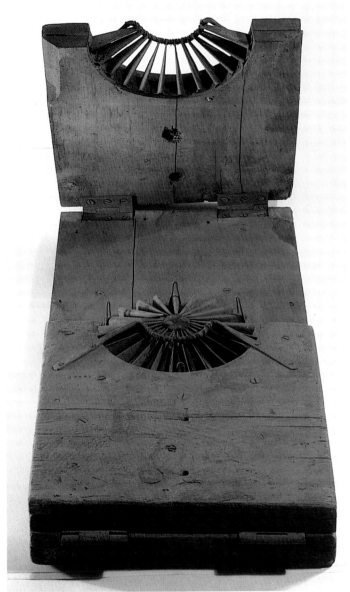

(TOP) *Hand-held shaping devices. Used by the glassmaker to insert into the 'mouth' of a trumpet shape and distort its rim into a series of folds, particularly small lighting shades and the small fluted containers from table centres. Royal Brierley Crystal, c. 1885.*

Royal Brierley Crystal Ltd. Photo, David Jones.

(ABOVE) *The use of the hand-held boliver to distort the edges of a blown form. Although these small devices operate on the same principles as the larger, floor-mounted ones, they are clearly only appropriate for small items. Once the glass has been puntied and opened, its rim and adjacent area are re-heated to soften them, and then pushed on to the fins of the boliver. These either catch or fold the glass to create the characteristic crimped form.*

A crimping boliver made of wood and brass. A rare example of the type of device made by the workshop facilities within one of the handmade glass factories during the late 19th century. It was almost certainly made in response to a design idea from within the factory and was clearly not robust enough to survive much contact with hot glass. It was probably a test rig produced to create a trial object before the expense of a permanent cast-iron device such as the one shown in the lower picture overleaf.

Royal Brierley Crystal Ltd. Photo, David Jones.

(ABOVE) *Crimped jug and holder. The use of devices such as the ones shown in the left-hand column of the previous page created the characteristic pleated surfaces. The jug and holder represent two stages of glassmaking, the jug being a blown bubble and the holder an opened out bubble.*

(OPPOSITE PAGE ABOVE) *Crimped jug and holder separated. Stevens and Williams, late 19th century.*

Both Royal Brierley Crystal Ltd. Photo, David Jones.

Cast-iron crimping boliver. Three-part, one side open. Devices like this would have been ordered from a metal foundry when protracted use was envisaged. A rig like this would have an indefinite lifespan.

Royal Brierley Crystal Ltd. Photo, David Jones.

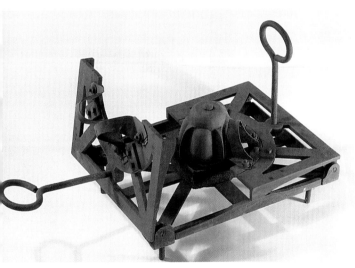

(ABOVE) *A lamp boliver. A standard device that was used to distort circular blown glass shades into the series of soft pleats and curves so characteristic of Victorian light fittings.*

Royal Brierley Crystal Ltd. Photo, David Jones.

(RIGHT) *Glass being blown into the lamp boliver. The glass is puntied, opened up, warmed, and pushed into the device. The two wings are closed to push the soft glass over the central shaper, and folded by fins arranged in relation to it.*

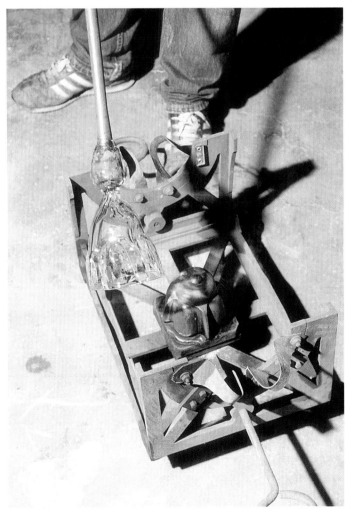

(RIGHT) *Dish and plate distorted on a lamp boliver. Stevens and Williams, late 19th century.*

(BELOW) *Moss-Agate: another use of an evocative name to reinforce the identity of the speciality glass techniques developed during the late-Victorian search for new glass product identities, much of which was achieved through the growing use of glass technology. The internal cracking that was the main feature of Moss-Agate derived from the combination of two types of glass within the same object, thereby ensuring that the weaker one cracked. It is also illustrative of the use of glass for purely decorative as opposed to practical forms. Made by Stevens and Williams in the 1880s.*

Both photos Broadfield House Glass Museum.
Photos, David Jones.

*A decorative item that has, in addition to being bolivered and pincered, been made in a specially
formulated colour glass. The exotic names given to these special colours, and which were often
patented, show the extent to which they were part of a marketable identity.
Made by Thomas Webb in 1900.*
Broadfield House Glass Museum. Photo, David Jones.

An example of the famous Silveria ware by Stevens and Williams in 1882. New effects and styles appeared to be the only way to gain commercial advantage, and considerable creative energy went into the development of these. Decorative processes such as silveria required great ingenuity and made full use of the vocabulary of hand skills available to the designers. A rough 'bag' of silver leaf, of the approximate shape of the vase, was picked up on a blown bubble, coated with another layer of glass mixed with coloured glass (trails and powder), gently inflated, puntied, sheared and given its final form. The silver, slightly torn by inflation, remains as a reflective surface within the glass.
Broadfield House Glass Museum. Photo, David Jones.

The development of heat-striking glasses that changed colour when re-heated was given a new dimension in this goblet through using a traditional technique. The use of a dip-mould created a series of regular protuberances on the blown bubble which, when re-heated in the gloryhole, absorbed more heat than the body of the glass and changed colour. Made in 1900 by Thomas Webb using uranium in the glass batch.

Broadfield House Glass Museum. Photo, David Jones.

(ABOVE) *Dish blown into a pierced copper frame. The fact that glass can be blown into a metal cage that both acts as a mould and becomes part of the finished piece has been known since Roman times. Here it is exploited for its purely decorative qualities. Note the way the shape and size of the apertures govern the extent to which the glass protrudes as it expands into and through the frame. Marked 'Cobral Ware', early 20th century, Broadfield.*
Broadfield House Glass Museum. Photo, David Jones.

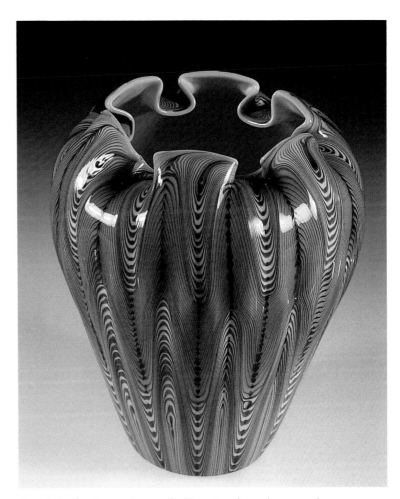

Vase created by the use of the pull-up device. The distortion in the horizontal rods has been further manipulated during the blowing of the body and the rotation involved in the manufacture of the rim and neck.

Broadfield House Glass Museum. Photo, David Jones.

Double 'pull-up' vase. Just as the Egyptian glassmakers created a different pattern by combing the horizontal lines from two different directions, so the device has been used to create the same feathered effect, probably by inserting the bubble twice. The rim has been distorted by the use of a boliver.

Broadfield House Glass Museum. Photo, David Jones.

(OPPOSITE PAGE BELOW)
John Northwood's pull-up machine and two vases decorated using it (above). Stevens and Williams 1884. Typical of the Victorian love of inventions this is a semi-mechanical version of the manual combing of horizontal threads used by glassmakers from ancient Egypt onwards. The machine was used in combination with his threading machine which completely covered the glass in horizontal rows of coloured threads. The bubble was placed in the device and inflated to bring the protruding threads into contact with the vertical saw teeth. These were moved up by using the hand wheel under the device, thereby creating distortions in the thread pattern.

Royal Brierley Crystal Ltd. Photo, David Jones.

NOVELTY COLOURS AND EFFECTS

The emergence of a scientifically based glass technology allowed the development of spectacular colours and surface effects to add to the repertoire of shape and texture, and became an integral part of the glass object. The new control and repeatability bestowed on the designer by technology allowed the active design of new types of glass. Colours that could be made to change selectively when re-heated uninhibited search for richness. The creative frenzy died out with the reaction to its, sometimes mindless, excesses (see pp 160, 161, 162, 163 and the top pictures on p.164).

A jug decorated with horizontal threading applied using a mechanical threading machine. The machine was really a device operated by a handle that bolted on to the glassmaker's chair and applied a hand-gathered blob of glass evenly by pulling it continually round the form. Its advantage over purely manual threading was the mechanical nature of the application (essential if the 'pull-up' was to be used). Made by Stevens and Williams in 1886.
Broadfield House Glass Museum. Photo, David Jones.

An enamelled jug – designed by Royal Academician Richard Redgrave, for Richardson's of Stourbridge in 1854. This was an attempt to re-invigorate traditional, expensive, hand-applied enamel painting through the addition of high-quality design. Although beautiful, it represents one of the last attempts to produce a commercial range of enamelled glass by hand. Hand decoration survived by becoming part of the expressive use of glass as a medium by named individuals like Gallé.

Broadfield House Glass Museum. Photo, David Jones

(ABOVE LEFT) *A distorting mould operated by an outside ring which is pushed up and down to open and close the brass arms. Unlike bolivers that are designed to shape the rim area, this type of device was used to partially shape the original bubble by distorting its surface into undulations that were reminiscent of rock crystal carvings.*

(ABOVE RIGHT) *The same 'rock-crystal' mould in the open position. Note the position of the outside ring.*

Both picures Royal Brierley Crystal Ltd. Photos, David Jones.

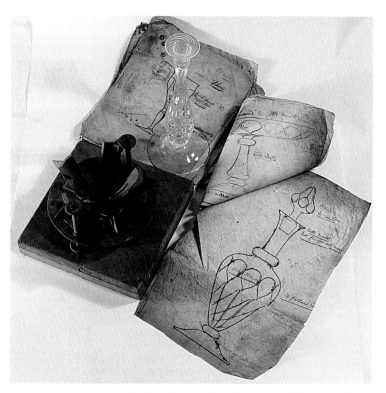

A 'rock-crystal' distorting mould with an object blown into it and the original glass-house drawings of a finished decanter. The surface pattern caused by the mould can be clearly seen.

Royal Brierley Crystal Ltd. Photo, David Jones.

THE NEW DESIGNERS

This aesthetic movement was led, in Britain, by designers like William Morris and Christopher Dresser and by writers like John Ruskin. When Dr Dresser was asked to design a range of blown glass decorative items for Coupers of Glasgow in 1885 he asked them to deliberately contaminate the glass to achieve a muddy, streaked and bubbled glass that resembled the murky waters of the Clyde. He specified that the objects blown from it should remain undecorated either hot or cold (see right). Tiffany on the other hand looked for a solution in a different direction. The glass designed and produced under his direction utilised the reputation of his family firm of jewellers, producing glass that was distinctly exclusive and upmarket. The way in which he developed iridescent effects (by employing a chemist) after being inspired by ancient glass he saw in a museum and which had developed iridescent surfaces after centuries of decay, epitomises the difference between the slow empiricism of glass development prior to the industrial era, and the self conscious search for particular effects in the modern era. Although he did not actually make glass or even design a great deal (preferring to employ in-house designers) Tiffany acted as an artistic director, ensuring that the products that bore his name maintained a particular standard and style. He also exploited the metalwork facilities and expertise available to him from the original jewellery wing of

(ABOVE) *Vase from the 'Finlandia' series by Timo Sarpaneva for Iittala 1964. Sarpaneva developed a method of mould making from carved and fired alderwood. As a result each time the mould was blown into the grain texture changed causing each object in the range to be unique although mould-blown.*

A free blown item from the Clutha range designed by Christopher Dresser for Couper & Sons, Glasgow, between 1890 and 1895. His deliberate specification of a glass contaminated with striations and bubbles in a single colour can be seen as a reaction to the sweet colouring and complex decoration of much late Victorian glass. He insisted that the glass and simple, hot making procedure be allowed to provide the full decorative impact of the form without recourse to secondary, applied decorative techniques. In this he was a forerunner of the 'truth to materials' movement of the 20th century.

Tiffany and Company. This created such hybrid masterpieces as the famous lamps with their bronze bases and leaded shades made up of pieces of Tiffany glass with their astonishing range of effects. Incidentally these lamps were designed to soften the harsh light given off by Edison's new incandescent light bulb. These lamps in particular and Tiffany glass in general illustrate a basic fact about the constant development of glass. Throughout its long history glass has flourished when cross-fertilised through contacts with new materials and technologies.

René Lalique approached glass initially from the same direction as Tiffany, jewellery. Originally one of the pre-eminent jewellers of the Art Nouveau period he moved effortlessly to address a new material, glass, and made an equally large contribution to the 20th century and Art Deco, as he had to the old. In terms of process and material Lalique's major contribution was to exploit the novel mass production process language of the new press and blow compressed air machines as a

(ABOVE) *A piece by the Scandinavian artist/designer Oiva Toikka,* Lollipop Isle, *made by Nuutajarvi, Finland, 1969. A purely sculptural piece that dramatically demonstrates the nature of glass and its manufacture. The freedom from practicality allowed designers to experiment with the glass and to incorporate the results into their individual creations. Allowing work like this to be made in a factory situation was one aspect of the collaboration with artist/designers who also designed functional ware.*
Courtesy of the trustees of the Victoria and Albert Museum. Photo, Daniel McGrath

designer. Producing relatively cheap objects (scent bottles for major perfume houses like Coty and Worth) which exude quality by virtue of their inventive design. The examples set by the association of well known, named designers with a particular range of products created a model of practice that was followed by the producers of high quality series artefacts. Particularly in Scandinavia (see right-hand column on previous page, above, opposite and pp. 168 and 169) the identities of the separate factories

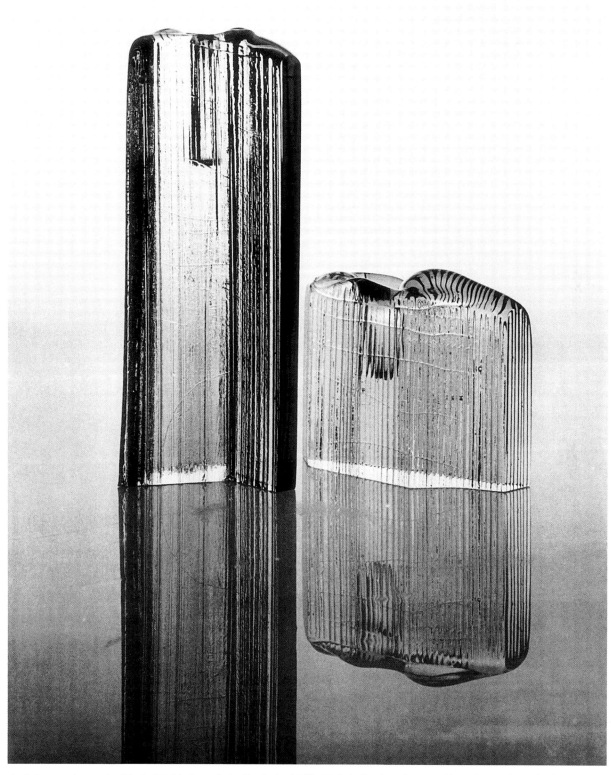

Paader's Ice: *sculptures by Tapio Wirkkala made by Iittala in 1962. Technically these forms could not be simpler – the form and texture derive from the interplay between the molten glass, the mould into which it is poured, and the pressure exerted to create the basic hollows in the top surface. The result is a magnificent example of a design that allows the material to speak for itself.*

(ABOVE) *A variation of the Graal technique in a piece by Eva Englund. The image is still created by sandblasting, but in this case by removing layers of cased colour. The form is still re-heated and covered with a clear layer of glass, but there is not enough depth to create a bubble. The pattern is created instead in colour alone.*
Broadfield House Glass Museum. Photo, David Jones.

(OPPOSITE PAGE) *An example of the Graal technique developed at Orrefors, Sweden, from 1916 onwards. It is a complex multi-staged process which is only really suitable for one-off exclusive products. A deep image is sandblasted into the surface of a vase shape that has already been formed and allowed to cool. This form is re-heated, picked up on a punty iron and covered in a layer of clear glass. This traps air in the pockets created by sandblasting and the image becomes delineated in bubbles.*
Broadfield House Glass Museum. Photo, David Jones

have become synonymous with the names of the designers they employ. The relationship is a particular one, more of a collaboration than that of employer and employee. Much store is laid on the individual nature of the designer who is given time and facilities to develop and exhibit highly personal work in addition to designing for commercial production. The way in which craft production has managed to survive has meant that great stress has been placed on the relationship between process and material in a creative, form giving sense. 'Truth to materials' is an oversimplification but does capture some of its essence. The creative energy of the designer has often been directed at devising new ways of shaping glass, that by their nature impart a character to its form and texture without the need for further elaboration (see p.169). Despite its long history of creative exploitation glass has offered many new such opportunities to designers in the 20th century. This individualism of process and/or approach to the material has often become closely associated with the formal vocabulary and signature of named designers. For example, Timo Sarpaneva's use of wooden moulds, and the development of the graal technique. Alvar Aalto's use of steamed wooden moulds to produce his famous Savoy vase was a by-product of his equally famous bent wood furniture, and both derived from his experiments with the new technology.

THE CENTRIFUGE

Most of these new ways of shaping glass were driven by aesthetics, and were very much part of the style movements of the early 20th century. Few were, technically, more than variants of, or additions to, well established craft traditions and their practices. Given the way in which craft based industries were forced to identify and market their products it is hardly surprising that this was the case. Also, as I have tried to point out, genuinely new glass processes are rare within its history and in the modern era these have been almost exclusively confined to machine, rather than craft based industries. However there are exceptions of which the centrifuge is the most notable. Although developed as a mass production process for light

fittings it has also been used effectively within the decorative craft based sector. In some ways the development of the glass centrifuge is one of the most original ways of shaping glass ever devised. Despite the fact that it starts from the same basic premise as all molten glass processes, liquidity, surface skin and elasticity, it approaches these from a new direction. Centrifugal force is employed to force the glass up the walls of a mould to shape it, and by the time the glass has lined the mould it has cooled and solidified enough to be removed and annealed. The process is triggered by spinning the mould at many thousands of revolutions per minute to create the necessary centrifugal force. A great advantage of this process is the way in which objects can be produced very quickly, a blob of molten glass can be converted into a finished vessel in a very short time. However, its formal characteristics are distinctive and result in qualities that are unique to it. A major feature of it is the way in which the liquid glass travels up the mould, and particularly the way in which it reacts to any protrusions in the mould's surfaces. Like any moving liquid its flow is deterred by raised areas and encouraged by hollows. As a result the eventual shape of the hollow vessel is affected by the ways in which the surface modelling and textures of the mould are organised. The rim of a centrifuged vessel displays the results of the journey the liquid glass has taken up the walls of the mould. This behavioural trait has been capitalised on by designers, and domestic objects produced by this method are often characterised by the way this has been exploited for decorative effect.

NEW GLASS TYPES

This portion of glass production, high quality, stylistic domestic ware, though important is only small in comparison with the volume of glass produced for other market segments, let alone for scientific, engineering and architectural purposes. It is remarkable that the scientific basis for a full control of glass manufacture, and therefore the ability to design glass types that will perform to specific and often contradictory specifications, is scarcely more than a century old. The control this understanding has given, has allowed science to counteract what have long been presumed basic glass characteristics. Coating glass with minute amounts of titanium has sealed the fragile surface where cracks begin, and increased its tensile strength dramatically. By varying its ingredients, its making circumstances and manufacturing conditions, the new technologists in charge of glass have the ability to literally design versions to order, selecting properties almost at will. For this reason glass is used across the full range of human activities, and can take a potentially infinite number of guises. Even this is not the end of the story. The development of hybrids of glass and other materials, notably ceramic, has created an entirely new genus of material. Glass ceramics have the major virtue of heat resistance and a minimal expansion coefficient. They can also be cast, cut and moulded to any configuration, hence their use in the space programme. The fact that glass is a supercooled liquid and a solution rather than a compound allows this constant development to take place. The fact that its basic constituent, silica, is one of the few materials the planet is in no danger of running out of, and its eminent recyclability not only guarantees its future but also indicates an ever widening role in the service of humankind.

CHAPTER SEVEN

Glass as an Art Material

'Of all the arts I know, none are more adventuresome, more uncertain, hence nobler than the arts invoked by fire.'

Paul Valery

Craft working, i.e. the shaping of materials by manually driven means using the workmanship of risk rather than certainty was, up to our own era, simply the only means available to shape materials and make things. Prior to the revolutionary impact of the centralised power sources that allowed the development of machines, craft procedures were adapted, as much as was possible, to maximise the skill available. Activities were organised to enable some level of standardisation, through a division of labour within teams of workers. The glassmaking team with the highly skilled gaffer at its centre exemplified this type of craft organisation. The skill of the gaffer was maximised by the team of up to five, lesser skilled workers who, by their simple, repeated actions saved him from unnecessary procedures, thereby concentrating the impact of his skill. Even within the craft based system the use of jigs, moulds and manually operated semi-automatic devices like the aptly named 'mechanical boy'[39] all speeded the process of making, and helped to standardise the products. Despite this the industry was still dependent on hard won craft skills, and ripe for the kind of product stripping made possible by the development of machine methods. The fact that craft making survived in any form into the 20th century is a tribute to the adaptability of glass and the creativity of the individuals who worked it.

ART GLASS

I have already described briefly how the craft manufacture of glass survived by exploiting the one area left to it, the handmade ethos in the production of expensive stylistic objects, but this was not the only way in which craft glassmaking re-invented itself. In common with a whole range of craft manipulated materials, ceramic, wood and metal, glass shifted from function to art in the hands of particular individuals. The movements dominated by the crafts in the developed world, that accompanied the first great machine age, all saw major stylistic contributions from glassmakers, Art Nouveau, Arts and Crafts, Jugendstyl all found some of their highest expression in that material. Individuals of great originality saw within the material vocabulary of glass a conduit for individual expression. Glass became for such people as much a medium as bronze or oil paint; practitioners like Gallé saw themselves as artists and their products as art. I do not intend to retell the already well known and documented account of studio based glass. Rather I am attempting to explain the major contribution made to this movement by the special nature of glass.

(OPPOSITE PAGE)

A sculptural form by the contemporary German glass artist, Jorg Zimmerman. It relies for much of its effect on the way glass is blown into and through a metal mesh cage that distorts the inflating bubble, breaking it into geometric pockets. The metal remains embedded as part of the final form.

Broadfield House Glass Museum. Photo, David Jones.

I have already mentioned the rather odd fact that, prior to our own era it was customary for one set of forming methods to dominate it to the exclusion of others. Our own era, by contrast, has been characterised by its use of the entire historical range of processes at the same time. This is of course, only true in the sense of glass as an expressive medium and has involved the re-discovery and renaissance of many dormant or lost processes. The impetus for this was provided by those individuals who sought a partnership with the material in the discovery and expression of their unique artistic voice. Whereas glass, during the vast bulk of its history, was employed anonymously in the service of society at large, it now became an essential active part of its maker's individual signature. There were two main sources that fed this development, one being the increasing knowledge of, and access to, glass from previous eras, the other being the emergence of the Artist/Maker.

THE INFLUENCE OF THE PAST

Archaeology provided sudden and dramatic examples of previously unknown objects and imagery. The first exhibitions of Egyptian art and artefacts in Europe in the 19th century caused a sensation that is impossible to fully comprehend today. Private and public collections displayed their objects in circumstances that allowed close personal study, and yet, because of their closed cases, stressed the purely stylistic and visual aspects of those objects. By stripping them of their original cultural significance and practical context they could only be viewed and appreciated in visual terms. Many artists felt inspired through close study and experiment to emulate these qualities and to absorb them into their own, expressive use of the medium. This new appreciation and appropriation of historical artefacts and processes was itself part of a larger movement, one that provided the other source from which the modern craft movement sprang. A growing group of individual artist/craftworkers broke down the prejudice against the working of craft materials themselves by anyone with any pretensions to academic standing or social status. In Western society the production of purely functional items by hand work was seen as a menial pursuit. The fine arts were exempted, as the nature of their end products implied intellectual overtones. The elevation of hand-driven systems like wheel throwing (ceramic) or glass blowing to activities with an intellectual rationale required them to be stripped of their practical, workplace associations. In any case the redefinition of craft methods was made both possible and necessary by their replacement by mechanisation. The objects made by the new breed of artist/maker served decorative and artistic ends and helped to convert materials like glass and ceramic into accepted expressive media. This realignment despite its beginnings in the second half of the 19th century, is still far from complete and a full convergence of art and craft has still to take place.

THE ARTIST/MAKER

The emergence of the artist/maker in glass (as in a number of other materials) was of a subtly different order to that of the artist/designer like Tiffany or even Gallé or Lalique. They functioned as leaders of teams or organisations. Lalique's drawings, for example, clearly demonstrate that his original ideas were intended to be interpreted by craftsmen. A single item often needing the combined expertise of a number of specialists to make it. Gallé recognised this in his use of his signature, and although he viewed himself as an artist he clearly created a hierarchy of production within his factory depending on how much he personally had to do with each piece. He only personally signed objects that he had worked on himself (although this was confined to the surfaces of pieces blown under his supervision). Objects made within his factory that did not pass through his hierarchy do not command the same contemporary value placed on works from his own hands. Although designer/makers like Gallé helped to revolutionise the perception of glass as a material there remains an important difference between his model of practice and that of artist/craftsmen like Francois Decorçhement. Gallé worked from a studio set within his factory, others went an important step further and brought all aspects of making into their studios. In doing so they helped to establish a studio craft tradition that is still evolving.

STUDIO-BASED GLASS

When, in 1888, C.R. Ashbee dedicated his translation of Cellini's Renaissance treatise to those 'who seek to find the meaning for their existence in the work of their own hands' he recognised and anticipated the attraction of actual, physical control over all aspects of an object's production. A satisfaction that has helped to support the emergence of a world wide craft movement that is sustained at every level of society. The way in which glassblowing, for instance, is now found within University faculties world wide is a direct result of the assimilation of the crafts by the intellectual elite begun over a century ago. The role played by the material in this shift has been a central one, as evidenced by the interest in both ancient techniques and the development of new ones (see below). Even within groupings of practitioners who appear to employ the same process, personal variants of the basic procedures are common. This is entirely consistent with the use of glass and its processes as a vehicle for individual expression.

A detail of a blown and cut item from the Hot Coral *series by Stuart Garfoot. The glass has been built up through successive gathers of contrasting colours, red, clear and black. This was blown into a contoured mould to create a relief pattern on the surface. On cooling the highest sections of the pattern were removed by grinding and polishing to reveal the first layer of red glass through the clear layer. This technique, whereby contrasting layers of glass cover each other, is as old as blowing (see the Portland vase) but here it is given a totally new character by the designer.*

Photo, Stuart Garfoot.

THE PERSONALISATION OF PROCESS

This can be seen in a process like *pâte-de-verre*, one which made such a major contribution to the establishment of glass as a medium of choice for French artist/craftsmen in the late 19th century. It was inspired by the qualities of Egyptian cast and core-formed glass but required a long period of experiment and development before it could be exploited as a stable, repeatable process. The experimental work of Henri Cros was spread over many years and comprised entirely of trial and error as a, personal, hands-on enquiry. The term he coined for the basic process of firing and fusing crushed glass within moulds in a kiln is not particularly descriptive, and in any case it became a number of variants of the generic principle in the hands of the small number of artists who used it. Each practitioner developed a personal way of organising and carrying out the stages that made up the total process. In doing so they stressed and exploited the aspects of it that were most closely related to their particular aesthetic viewpoint. To this extent they can be said to have taken the material into partnership in their creative endeavour. This could only have been achieved within a model of practice that placed the choice and development of glass process (literally) in the hands of the artist craftsman. It is therefore impossible to divorce the *pâte-de-verre* work of someone like G. Argy-Rousseau from his highly personalised version of it. The surfaces and precise disposition of detail and colour, which characterise his pieces, could only have been achieved through the use of the complex and painstaking methods he devised, and which he described in his personal notebooks. The technique itself had been brought about originally through the influence and example of ancient glassworks that were created using cast glass grains. However, the individuals involved in its rebirth rapidly went far beyond the very basic processes used in the ancient world.

GLASS AS A FINE-ART MATERIAL

The fact that the objects made by the new artist-craftsmen were signed by them in the manner of Fine Art was itself symptomatic of the revolution in glass use and perception. Moving the activity from a workshop to a personal studio also helped to convert the material and the physical movements that shaped it into an expressive and intellectual pursuit. This was absolutely essential if the glass products of this system were to be taken seriously as signature art works, and eventually, to become valued as highly as painting and sculpture. This was the only way in which the use of glass as an artistic medium could contribute to the furtherance of time-consuming hand processes in the first machine age. It is interesting to note that such ways of making were relevant to the Ancient World where their non functional use in the creation of ritual objects supported their long winded, labour intensive methods. The coming of the new Roman order, and the conversion of glass to a material from which to produce containers in large quantities saw both the object types and their production methods eclipsed by the new economic imperatives. Yet the same processes enjoyed a rebirth in the period that accompanied mass production. Despite the fact that this was due to their use in art associated products, attempts were made by Argy Rousseau (see opposite) and Amalric Walter to rationalise such production by the employment of small workshops and limited series manufacturing runs of near identical objects. The intention, of course, was to speed up manufacture and thereby increase sales, but a variety of factors militated against their success. Argy Rousseau, who employed twenty people to make editions of his *pâte-de-verre* creations, called himself an industrialist yet boasted that no two pieces of his work were the same. Despite the use of moulds to cast the glass, editions rarely exceeded fifty of any one shape, making for a total output during ten years of between fifteen and twenty thousand items.

THE LEGACY OF THE ARTIST-CRAFTSMEN

The success of these pioneer glass artists must be measured in terms of the sheer quality of their objects, and the way in which their example helped to establish such practice as a serious artistic and intellectual pursuit. Their dual legacy lies in the way their work is prized and displayed in museums and major collections, and in the fact that studio glass

A pâte-de-verre *shade produced in Argy-Rousseau's workshop in the 1920s. Despite the fact that each mould had to be packed with glass grains by hand, and the mould was destroyed in the production of a single item, Rousseau attempted series manufacture. The way in which his version of the basic* pâte-de-verre *process allowed such an accurate disposition of colour within the form is testament to his greatness. The highlights have been emphasised by brush polishing with fine pumice powder.*

has become a major feature of the contemporary craft movement. Although the work of most of the early glass artists was brought to a halt by the First World War their model of studio based glass production was continued by a new generation. In glass terms the most important of these was undoubtedly Maurice Marinot (see a piece of his work on p. ii), who took the new approach to the medium back into the glass factory, but in doing so claimed glassblowing and hot glass manipulation as viable artistic methods. Marinot was a well known painter of the *fauve* group who became excited by the possibilities offered by glass as a potential medium when he visited a glass factory. His first efforts were based on the decoration of simple blown forms (that were made for him) using acid and enamelling. These early pieces display a painter's use of technique in their bold formal designs, e.g. his original and radical use of acid etching to totally re-shape the vessel sculpturally. However, he realised that in order to truly use glass as an expressive medium he would have to learn to shape hot glass himself by acquiring a mastery of the traditional skills of glassblowing. He invested the required time and energy (many years) to gain these skills and then used them in the service of his own essentially painterly, vision. Although artists like Cros, Argy-Rousseau and Decorçhement had already made this journey from craft to art their chosen route was through casting rather than engaging in a physical, direct dialogue with glass. The skills of glassblowing became totally integrated into his aesthetic vision and vocabulary of form. This is perhaps best demonstrated by his invention and use of special tools with which he manipulated the molten glass. The results are works of art whose presence are totally bound up with the manner of their individual production. Marinot started as an artist who painted and he remained an artist, merely changing his preferred medium from paint to glass. In doing so he also changed the course of glass as a medium, and the fact that today, worldwide, hundreds of students study glass at degree level, through glassblowing, is a fitting tribute to his example. True to his individual nature Marinot did not have apprentices or even direct followers, and his own practice was cut short by the Second World War. Nevertheless by this time his work had been recognised and judged by the criteria he had wanted, as highly valued works that expressed the creativity of a gifted individual artist. Marinot died in 1960.

His example inspired other European artists to work in the same way, Erwin Eisch for example; but perhaps the most important development was the post-war craft movement begun in America. This involved the establishment of a large scale, multi-media approach to the crafts, one that came to be supported by a number of allied systems, education, galleries, publications, critics and theorists, all of which ensured its survival and spread (see p. 178). Western European notions of craft materials and practices, with their traditional legacy of low status, and tainted by the ghost of practicality were ignored in America in an outburst of post-war optimism. The traditional European term 'ceramic', with its associations of work and function, was replaced by the more neutral 'clay work'. The important tenet of the new approach was the absolute insistence on the manual working of the chosen material. Those who chose glassblowing as their method would go to extraordinary creative lengths to avoid a reliance on an assistant, such was the strength of the individual ethos. Another characteristic of the American movement that was to spread worldwide, was the search for originality of form, and allied to this, the development of an individual contribution to forming methods. In many successful practitioners' works the nature of their signature shapes, colours, patterns and textures are so bound up with their particular methods of shaping glass as to be synonymous. The work and career of Joel Phillip Myers displays this, with, for example, his 'fragments' series resulting from the highly original techniques developed by him to lay shards of glass on the surface of his blown vessel forms.

The early experiments of Harvey Littleton, Dominick Labino and Erwin Eisch were geared to the design of a practical studio furnace as a source of workable hot glass. Their success enabled hot glass working to break its dependence on factory scale facilities, and move into studios and educational establishments where they were worked experimentally, and within a looser and broader theoretic and material context. The title of Harvey Littleton's book, *Glassblowing, a search for form* describes

A sculptural piece by the American artist Michael Glancy. In his work, Glancy exploits the technique of sandblasting to erode the surfaces of his blown glass forms, and follows this by electro-depositing a layer of metal (in this case, copper) into the depressions. He makes use of the fact that glass is a poor conductor of electricity and can therefore be selectively sensitised to carry the necessary charge to allow the deposition of metals.
Serpentine Star X. Blown glass and copper.
Photo, Gene Dwiggins.

the approach particularly of the 1960s, precisely. It also demonstrates the way in which this approach differs from that of the designer craftsman. In Littleton's model the end product is the result of an open-ended, creative dialogue between maker and material, and although many of the pieces made during this period look relatively crude and naïve today, their true importance must be judged in terms of what effect their example has exerted on subsequent generations. Since the early tentative, but enthusiastic, steps of the 1960s the studio glass movement has spread in less than four decades across the world (see opposite). The

A sculptural group by the American artist Rick Mills, using the organic vocabulary of blowing for purely sculptural purposes. Inflation is utilised to create shapes rather than containers. These have been combined with wrought iron.

A glass 'event' by the Swedish artist Bertil Vallien. The excitement generated by the sight of hot mobile glass is used by Vallien. A metal container full of liquid glass is lifted above a tray of casting sand. The base is removed and the glass allowed to pour through a perforated plate. The streams become a mass of fine filaments. The performance value of hot glass has been a feature of its use by individual artists since the growth of the studio glass movement in the mid-20th century.
Bertil Vallien.

fact that it is the strongest in developed, post-industrial societies is a tribute to both its processes and the nature of its end products. To be in total control of a material and its craft methods is a satisfying and relatively rare experience in a post-industrial age, and accounts for a large proportion of its attraction as a choice of occupation. The fact that objects produced by such individual methods, and in materials with a long history, have qualities that cannot be obtained in modern, mass-produced versions ensure their survival and continued evolution.

In particular the unique fusion of silica and ash that results in the synthetic material, glass, has, in addition to its separate identities in the service of science, engineering and architecture been accepted as a fully fledged artistic medium.

CHAPTER EIGHT

The Singularity of Glass

Almost any attempt to describe the special nature of glass will sooner or later employ the word 'unique', yet it is difficult to define exactly the nature of its singularity. This has much to do with the fact that if glass were merely unique it would be much less interesting, as this would imply that it was self-contained and somehow separate from other materials. In fact, one of its strongest characteristics has been its constant adaptation to new demands and the creative interplay with other materials and their technologies that has made this possible.

As I hope this book has established, it has few, if any, fixed qualities, whether in physical, chemical or aesthetic terms. It would seem that its uniqueness does not lie in this direction. It has been described as stone, metal and crystal by civilisations who manipulated its manufacture and use to anchor it within a particular material context.

Many materials have an inherent value, e.g. gold and pewter, that largely determines (and limits) the nature, scale, function and value of the objects made from them. By contrast glass has found expression at all levels of human endeavour from the tiny, highly valued beads and jewels of the Egyptians to the recent glass roof over the British Museum courtyard by Sir Norman Foster. It is at the same time the ideal material from which to mass produce ubiquitous, low-cost containers and the medium of choice for the artist and craftsman. Its value is determined by factors that exist outside its material identity and which decide whether objects fashioned from it are the equal of gold and precious stones or endlessly re-cycled via the bottle bank. Rarity is clearly a determinant as well as the quality and amount of skill used; the survival and display of the Portland vase in the British Museum (despite the vase's shattered condition) is a case in point. Glass does not reveal itself to any one age or group of specialists let alone to a single individual. Yet each seems to feel that their partial view captures the central essence of the material, be it transparency, fragility, or their opposites, strength or flexibility. Each age, group or individual uses only the small segment of glass's total repertoire that relates to their particular needs. Thanks to scientific research this already vast repertoire is constantly being added to, for if a glass with the precise specifications required does not exist it can be brought into being through novel variations of, or additions to, its basic mix, or through partnerships with other materials.

Its essential nature and its uniqueness lies, therefore, not in its properties, uses values or objects, for all of these are relative to the specific circumstances of its utilisation. Across each of these categories any apparent characteristic is immediately nullified by its exact opposite. Its uniqueness is the fact that it has and continues to be subject to constant re-figuring and re-definition, although this itself is merely a symptom of its special nature and not its actual source. This resides ultimately in the way the material is made, for it is the synthesis of ingredients by heat that provides a unique set of behavioural characteristics that allow it to be shaped. It is this that permits access to the myriad material properties and is the key to its use and its constant regeneration.

Notes

1   Gloria Hickey, *Craft within a Consuming Society: Culture of the Crafts.*

2   S. Frank, *Glass and Archaeology*, Academic Press, 1982

3   Glass is now defined as a Post-Newtonian solid.

4   R.W. Douglas and S Frank, *A History of Glassmaking*, Foulis, 1972

5   P.T. Nicholson, *Egyptian Glass and Faience*, Shire 1993

6   Ada Polak, *Glass, Its Makers and Public,* London, 1975

7   P.T. Nicholson, *Egyptian Faience and Glass*, 1993

8   Carried out by Colin Reid at Stourbridge College of Art in 1981.

9   The trading vessel went down off the coast of Turkey in the 14th century BC.

10 Probably a polished marble slab. *Marver* is derived from the Latin name for Marble.

11 E.G. Fish. British Museum *EA 55193*

12 Our true appreciation of the use of glass during the Mesopotamian era is hampered by the fact that its products did not survive well. In contrast, Egyptian glass artefacts have been preserved by the geographic and climatic conditions.

13 In the Cairo Museum.

14 The glass block, measuring 3.4 m x 1.95 m and weighing 9 tonnes found at Bet She 'Arim, Israel, is now dated to the 9th century AD but is accepted as part of a tradition of manufacture that produced large amount of glass for trade as ingots. See *Journal of Glass Studies*. Vol. VI.

15 Quoted from Dan Klein, *The History of Glass*, Orbis, 1989.

16 Small diameter tube production clearly did exist (see p.47). It is the scale of tubing necessary for container blowing that I doubt, not the principle.

17 Whitefriars Glass Company moved to Wealdstone in 1923 from its premises in central London, where it had operated for 200 years. To emphasise the continuity the new furnaces were lit from a flame ceremoniously carried between the old and new sites.

18 Where wood remained the prime fuel, fritting was essential. St Gobain for example did not convert from wood until the 19th century.

19 Huizinga, *Homo Ludens*, Paladin, 1970.

20 Diary entry for 23rd October 1663.

21 *The Nature and Art of Workmanship*, Pye, 2nd edition, London, Hebert Press, 1995

22 E.W. Fairfield, *Fire and Sand*, Cleveland, Ohio, 1960.

23 'Who Were the Glassmakers?' Kurinsky, *Glass Art Society Journal*, 1995

24 Paul Fossing, *Glass before Glassblowing*

25 It is important to draw a distinction between glass as an ancillary material, e.g. as a glaze for ceramic or stone, and as a material in its own right capable of supporting complete objects. 3000 BC is thought to be when it was used as a material in its own right.

26 R.N. Douglas and S. Frank, *A History of Glassmaking*, London, 1972

27 A.L. Oppenheim, *Glass and Glassmaking in Ancient Mesopotamia*, R. Brill, Corning, 1970

28 G.O. Jones, *Glass*, Chapman and Hall, 1971 (2nd ed)

29 It also allows gold leaf to be incorporated into the decoration. Venetian enamelled work of the 15th century would have been impossible without it. See *Glass Circle Journal*, Vol. 1, 1975

30 See Ada Polak, *Glass: Its Makers and Public*, Weidenfeld and Nicholson, London, 1975

31 Polak, op. cit.

32 'English Looking Glasses', Geoffrey Wills, *Country Life*,1965

33 Early records have been destroyed, but it must have been around 1830.

34 *History of Technology*, Vol. IV. Butterworth.

35 J.F. Chance, *A History of Chance Bros. and Co*, Spottiswoode, Ballantyne, 1919.

36 E.M. Ramsden, *The Story of the Glass Bottle*, Stoke-on-Trent, 1972.

37 The production in 1934 of the giant 200 inch glass reflector by Corning is a classic example. The fascinating story is told in a narrative form in *The Glass Giant of Palomar* by D.O. Woodbury, London, 1940.

38 Relative to production costs and the investment required to mechanise. In relation to other skilled workers glassblowers were among the better paid. See *The Aristocracy of Labour Revisited* by Takeo Matsumura, Manchester, 1991.

39 A two-part mould traditionally operated by a boy apprentice. The mechanical version operated it via a foot-operated pedal and allowed the gaffer to work it himself.

Bibliography

Bacri, C. Daum *Masters of French Decorative Glass*, Thames & Hudson, 1993

Bloch, Dermant and J.G. Argy-Rousseau *Glassware as Art*, Thames & Hudson, Paris, 1991

Bray, C. *Dictionary of Glass —Materials and Techniques*, (2nd ed.) A & C Black, London, 2001

Chance, J. F. *A History of Chance Bros and Co.*, Spottiswood, Ballantyne, l919

Charleston, R.J *Masterpieces of Glass*, Adams, New York, 1980

Douglas, R. W. and Frank, S. *A History of Glassmaking*, Foulis, 1972

Engle, F.A. *Reading in Glass History*, Phoenix, Jerusalem, 1977

Fossing, P. *Glass Vessels Before Glass Blowing*, Copenhagen, 1940

Frank, S. *Glass and Archaeology*, London, 1982

Fukai, S. *Persian Glass*, Weatherhill, New York, 1977

Gardi, R. *African Crafts and Craftsmen*, Van Nostrand Rheinhold, 1969

Garnier, P. *Emile Galle*, Academy, 1976

Giberson, D. F. *A Glassblowers Companion*, Joppa, 199

Goldstein, S. *Pre-roman and Early Roman Glass in the Corning Museum of Glass*, Corning, 1979

Hajdamack, C. *British Glass 1800–1914*, Antique Collectors Club, 1991

Haralson, C. *The Eloquent Object*, Philbrook Museum of Art, 87

Hardern, D. R. *Glass of the Caesars*, CAR, Milan, 1987

Jones G. O. *Glass*, Chapman and Hall, 1971

Klein, D. *Glass a Contemporary Art*, Collins, 1989

Klein, D. and Lock, W. *Glass*, Orbis, 1984

Kurinsky, S. *Who Were the Glassmakers?*, Glass Art Society Journal, 1995

Labino, P. *The Egyptian Sand-Core Technique*, Journal of Glass Studies VII, 1966

Layton, P. *Glass Art*, A & C Black, London, 1997

Lierke, R. *Glass Bowls Made on the Potters Wheel*, Glastech No. 12, 1991

Maloney, F. *Glass in the Modern World*, Aldus, London, 1967

Meigh, E. *The Story of the Glass Bottle*, Ramsden, 1972

Mumford, L. *Technics and Human Development*, London, 1967

Neuberg, F. *Ancient Glass*, London, 1967

Nicholson, P. T. *Egyptian Faience and Glass*, Shire, 1993

Opie, J. *Scandinavian Ceramics and Glass in the Twentieth Century*, Victoria And Albert Museum, 1989

Oppenheim, A. L. *Glass And Glassmaking in Ancient Mesopotamia*, Corning Museum of Glass Press, 1970 and 1988

Pellatt, A. *Curiosities of Glassmaking*, Boque, 1849

Petrova, S. and Olivie, J-L. *Bohemian Glass*, Flamniarion, 1989

Polak, A. *Glass Its Makers and Public*, Weidenfield & Nicholson, London, 1975

Polak, A. *Modern Glass*, Faber & Faber, London, 1962

Powell, H.J. *Glass Making in England*, Cambridge University Press, 1923

Revi, A. C. *Nineteenth Century Glass. Its Genesis and Development*, Nelson, 1968

Shand, E. B. *Glass Engineering Handbook*, McGraw-Hill, 1958

Singer, L. *A History of Technology*, Vols 1-5, Oxford, 1957

Spillman, J. S. *American and European Pressed Glass in the Corning Museum*, Corning Museum, 1981

Tate, H. *Five Thousand Years of Glass*, British Museum, London, 1991

Utt, M. and G. *Lalique Perfume Bottles*, Thames & Hudson, 1991

Wakefield, H. *Nineteenth Century British Glass*, Faber, 1961

Weiss, G. *The Book of Glass*, London, 1971

Index